The Autobiography of
CHARLES HALLÉ

The Autobiography of

CHARLES HALLÉ

With correspondence and diaries

Edited with an introduction by
Michael Kennedy

BARNES & NOBLE
BOOKS
10 East 53d St., New York 10022
(a division of Harper & Row Publishers, Inc.)

Published in the U.S.A. 1973 by:
HARPER & ROW PUBLISHERS, INC
BARNES & NOBLE IMPORT DIVISION

First published by Paul Elek Ltd, London, 1972

*The Life and Letters of Sir Charles Hallé: being an autobiography
(1819–1860) with correspondence and diaries* edited by
C. E. Hallé and Marie Hallé, was first published in
London, 1896.
This select edition and Editor's introduction and notes
copyright © 1972 by Paul Elek Ltd.

ISBN 06–493634–1

Printed in Great Britain

Contents

List of illustrations

Between pages 88 and 89

Between pages 136 and 137

Introduction

Music-making in Britain in the latter half of the nineteenth century was to a remarkable extent dominated by three foreign-born musicians. Each settled permanently in the land of his adoption and each was eventually knighted—three Eminent Victorians, one from Naples, one from Stolzenburg, one from Hagen, Westphalia. They were Sir Michael Costa (1808-84), conductor of the Italian Opera at Covent Garden, of the Philharmonic Society and of the Handel Festivals from 1857 to 1880; Sir August Manns (1825-1907), conductor of the Crystal Palace Concerts from 1855 to 1901; and Sir Charles Hallé (1819-95), founder of the Hallé Concerts in Manchester. Hallé's name and memory are kept green by the continuing fame and success of the Hallé Orchestra, and it may be argued that, of the three, his life-work was the most lasting and far-reaching in its effects upon the development of orchestral music and standards in Britain. The retention of the name Hallé for Manchester's orchestra is testimony in itself to the extraordinary power of this man's influence. So far as I know, only one other orchestra of comparable standard – the Paris Lamoureux – retains the name of its long-dead founder. There was no committee decision to name the Hallé Orchestra—Manchester's concerts for nearly fifty years had been known as 'Hallé's concerts' and so they remained after their founder had died. The strength of feeling about this can be gauged from a letter written to Hans Richter three years after Hallé's death by Frederic Cowen, who had been called in as 'stop-gap' conductor until Richter was free to leave Vienna for Manchester. Cowen fought to keep the post and wrote to

7

his proposed supplanter suggesting reasons why Richter would not be happy in Manchester. He gave one of them as 'the title of the Hallé Concerts and the Hallé Orchestra which the people will never consent to change.'

Hallé's personality—his urbane charm, his quiet humour and his total lack of pomposity—emerges very strongly from the pages of his autobiography. It was a calamitous loss for historians that he died when his narrative had reached only 1860, leaving thirty-five years of his career unchronicled. (But no doubt he would have become more reticent the nearer he came to the time at which he was writing.) It was published in 1896, with additional material by his eldest son Charles E. Hallé and his daughter Marie, together with a selection of letters and extracts from his diaries. It has not since been reprinted, but its racy style and candid approach, so different from many Victorian memoirs, merit its being again made available. The text is unaltered, but I have supplied a few footnotes. I have selected some letters and a diary fragment of 1855-56 from the 1896 edition, and placed this material at the end of relevant sections of the autobiography, thereby giving modern readers the opportunity of comparing Hallé's recollections written many years later with what he wrote at the time. Minor discrepancies cannot, I think, alter our impression of his remarkable memory. Finally, most of C. E. Hallé's 'postscript', covering the years 1865-95, is retained. We must take on trust (and I believe we may) C. E. Hallé's scrupulous fidelity to the originals of the diaries and letters, since none of them has ever been traced.

The making of the man is evident from the pages about his childhood. No tale of woe, this, of ambition frustrated or talent unrecognised, but a loving account of a truly happy family home, with wise and unpossessive parents, the joys of Christmas and New Year—the description of the nightwatchman must recall Act II of *Die Meistersinger* to all opera-lovers who read it—and a constant background of music. Hallé does not say, nor can it now be discovered, what was the cause of his delicacy as an infant, but he is but one of many illustrious men who have lived to an active and healthy old age after a shaky start. Nor does he tell us whether the Hallé family had been musicians before his father: one assumes from his narrative that his paternal and maternal grandparents were dead before he was born.

It is clear, however, that Hallé's father was the focal point of musical life in Hagen, as teacher and organist. This little town lacked the facilities of its neighbours such as Iserlohn and Dortmund. There was a small concert-hall, but no opera house. Yet Hallé records that music seemed to be Hagen's chief occupation,[1] with recitals and choral practices in private houses and such keenness to hear opera that a makeshift stage was built once a year in a hotel ballroom and the orchestra was provided by the town's amateurs. It is obvious, though, reading between the lines, that standards were on the low side. The really important feature of Hallé's days in Hagen in its effect on his adult career was the devotion of his father to the music of Beethoven. To take part at the age of seven in Beethoven's 'Archduke' Trio, op.97, in 1826 was no common experience. When he went to study in Darmstadt at the age of sixteen it was Beethoven's 'Eroica' Symphony, fully rehearsed, that made the deepest impression on him and on the orchestral players to whom it was evidently a novelty. This adoration of Beethoven's music lasted throughout Hallé's life, and it is fascinating to read his account of Chopin's reaction to the sonatas. It was Hallé's distinction to be the first pianist to play all the Beethoven sonatas for the first time in both Paris and London; and in Manchester, too, of course. He played the whole cycle of sonatas in London regularly until the last year of his life and he was practising the C minor concerto (no.3) on the

---

[1] It is worth recording that, in its centenary year 1958, the Hallé Orchestra conducted by Sir John Barbirolli gave a concert in Hagen. It was also at Hagen, in 1929, that Walton's *Façade* was first staged as a ballet.

evening of his death.

This brings us to consideration of how good a pianist Hallé was. His autobiography makes it clear that he was something of a prodigy by Hagen standards, but when he reached Paris he encountered difficulty in finding a teacher. Amid such a galaxy of talent—Liszt, Chopin and Thalberg, for examples—he felt himself to be at a disadvantage. His strength of character is shown by his vow not to appear in public in Paris for at least three years until he reached a level of achievement which satisfied his own criteria. He had nothing of the flashy virtuoso in his make-up—one is tempted to say he was too good a musician. Dazzled as he was by Liszt's piano-playing he was under no illusion about the vagaries of Liszt's taste and the liberties he took with other composers' music —although he was human enough, as he confesses and as Anton Schindler, Beethoven's friend and biographer, noted with horror, to emulate Liszt at one time, even to playing certain passages in the 'Emperor' concerto in octaves instead of in single notes. Hallé's *métier* seems to have been chamber music and the salon recital. His reputation might have been more sensational if he had not lived in an age when the influence of Liszt led so many others, lacking Liszt's genius, to ape the less worthy aspects of his style and character. So, by some critics, Hallé's playing was considered, by comparison, to be cold and scholarly, even dull. I suspect that Bernard Shaw's assessment of him when he was over seventy is nearer to a balanced judgment: 'Nobody who has heard him play the largo of this sonata [Beethoven's op.10 no.3 in D major] has ever accepted the notion that his playing is "icy and mechanical". Is there any audience in the world that would come to hear [Anton] Rubinstein play a Beethoven sonata for the 20th time? Yet Hallé . . . is always sure of his audience . . . The secret is that he gives you as little as possible of Hallé and as much as possible of Beethoven, of whom people do not easily tire.' Hallé's friend, the composer and pianist Stephen Heller, told him: 'You have remained my ideal as a pianist, for you never exaggerate.' Writing in the third edition of Grove's *Dictionary of Music and Musicians*, J. A. Fuller-Maitland suggested that in public Hallé did not always 'let his individuality of temperament come out. In private, the humour of his nature and the vivacity of his character, which he preserved all his life under a somewhat solemn aspect, gave to his performances a life and intellectual beauty which could not be forgotten. . . .'

If it is impossible for us to recall the actual quality of Hallé's piano-playing, it is easy to assess his extraordinary industry and adventurousness. At the vast majority of his Manchester concerts, almost all of which he conducted, he nearly always played a concerto and a group of piano solos—from 1850 to 1895! That takes no account of his many concerts, solo recitals and violin and pianoforte sonata recitals elsewhere. Nor did he keep to the same works. He had his favourites, of course, Beethoven especially, but in 1876 he played Grieg's concerto and when he was nearing sixty-four he played Brahms's B flat major concerto (the immense no.2) in Manchester only a few weeks after its first London performance and almost exactly a year after Brahms had given the first performance in Budapest on November 9, 1881. He played Dvořák's concerto in the autumn of 1885 and Tchaikovsky's second concerto in October 1886. It was an astonishing testimony to his apparent agelessness of mind and fingers.

Hallé's autobiography is to be treasured above all else for its brilliant if all too brief picture of artistic life in Paris at a time when, one can say without much fear of exaggeration, no city before or since has been the residence of so much genius and talent in so many fields. (Some of his letters, too, describe the city as it was in 1836 with a flair for detail.) The descriptions of Liszt and Chopin are invaluable coming not only from a friend but from a friend who was also a pianist. One senses the authenticity of every

11

word of the encounter with Paganini. How touching, too, is the picture of the three young men, Hallé, Heller and Wagner, writing a letter of admiration to Schumann after Hallé had played *Carnaval.* But the man who dominates these pages is Hector Berlioz, and it says much for the sheer musicianship which characterised Hallé that he at once appreciated his friend's genius and the genius of his music. Crucial here is the account of Habeneck's famous snuff-taking at a vital moment in the first performance of the *Requiem.* Hallé's version corroborates Berlioz's, except that with characteristic kindliness, he attributed Habeneck's action to carelessness whereas Berlioz, understandably and probably rightly, put it down to malice.

The friendship with Berlioz is of special significance in two respects: it led to Hallé's pioneering work in England for his music, and it must have planted in Hallé's mind the ambition to conduct. Tantalisingly, Hallé says nothing in his memoirs about what led him to take up conducting. It appears that apart from the childhood venture when he conducted opera in Hagen while his father was ill, he never picked up the baton in his life until we find him accepting the appointment as conductor of Manchester's Gentlemen's Concerts in 1850 at the age of thirty and setting about it with such confidence that he laid down very firm conditions about rehearsals and the engagement of players and with such success that he was soon engaged for seasons of opera. We learn from the memoirs that he was an assiduous attender of rehearsals both in Darmstadt and in Paris (especially Berlioz's) and it is reasonable to assume that he thereby learned a good deal about conducting. Shaw thought him a very fine conductor; Ernest Helme, a friend of James Agate, described Hallé's conducting as 'brilliant and fiery', adjectives which suggest the example of Berlioz. Fuller-Maitland wrote of Hallé imposing his will on his players 'with an amount of willpower that was unsuspected by the public at large.'

What the cause of Berlioz in Britain owes to Hallé can

easily be demonstrated. He conducted *Harold in Italy* in Manchester in 1855. Although he had settled in Manchester in 1848, it was not until ten years later that he launched his own series of concerts. In the very first programme on January 30, 1858 he included a short Berlioz item, the *Ballet des Sylphes* from *La Damnation de Faust.* Later in that first season came the slow movement from *Harold in Italy* and the *Carnaval Romain* overture. Evidently Hallé did not feel that his audience and his bank balance were yet ready for substantial Berlioz works and for several years he continued to dangle the carrot of short pieces before them: the *Queen Mab* scherzo, of course, and the Ball movement from the *Symphonie Fantastique.* He conducted the first complete performance in England of the *Fantastique* on January 9, 1879. He followed this on February 5, 1880, with the first performance in England of *La Damnation de Faust.* In the same year, on December 30, he conducted *L'Enfance du Christ*, also its first English performance, but although he repeated it twice in subsequent years it was never popular with the audience. Then, on December 29, 1881, he did a complete *Romeo and Juliet.* Some years later he even persuaded Edward Lloyd to sing a tenor song from *Lélio.* Of all these works, English taste in the late nineteenth century most favoured *Faust*, which soon became a popular work and which Hallé conducted many times throughout Britain. His championship of the other works met with a chilly reception. London cold-shouldered his Berlioz concerts in the early 1890s so disastrously that economics compelled him to abandon these annual visits.

This great Berlioz tradition has been maintained at the Hallé concerts. Even Hans Richter, who was so scornful of French music, conducted *Romeo and Juliet.* Cowen conducted *The Trojans at Carthage* in December 1897, and it was performed in Manchester again in 1928 by that superb Berliozian, Sir Hamilton Harty, who had conducted the *Requiem* in 1925, an event then of such rarity that the French critics travelled to Manchester to hear it. Beecham and Barbirolli also gave superb Berlioz performances in their Hallé concerts.

Yet this was only one aspect of Hallé's work in Manchester. It is still astonishing to imagine the contrast between the kind of life Hallé knew in Paris for twelve years and what he encountered in the North of England in 1848. Hardly less remarkable is the equanimity with which he faced the contrast, partly no doubt from necessity but mainly by his urbane temperament which one senses very strongly in all his writings, as when he confesses that he was 'attracted powerfully' to Manchester 'by the hope of fostering the taste for music in so large a community.' He had also, of course, to learn English, just as he had had to learn French when he went to Paris. He seems only to have faltered very slightly in the summer of 1850 when, as a letter to the critic H. F. Chorley indicates, he was tempted by the idea of settling in London. Eventually, he combined the best of both cities and had a London house.

Manchester in 1848 was very prosperous and at the zenith of its commercial enterprise. It was also horribly scarred by the causes of its prosperity—it is the Manchester of 1844 that Engels has unforgettably and accurately described, a city in which appalling squalor and poverty could be found a stone's throw from the ornate and substantial imitation *palazzi* which housed the cotton. Yet it was a city in which there was a lively if circumscribed cultural and social life. Manchester had long enjoyed a musical reputation—long before the Germans settled there for business reasons and encouraged it still further. Since about 1770 the town had boasted the Gentlemen's Concerts, named after the twenty-four amateur male flautists who met regularly in a tavern and whose activities developed into an orchestra for which a concert hall was built in 1777. These concerts were for subscribers only. Twelve were given each season, six choral and six instrumental and vocal, and the programmes regularly included symphonies by contemporary composers—

14

Haydn, Mozart and Beethoven. A considerable amount of musical activity was encouraged by 'the gentry' who lived in the district: Sir Thomas Egerton and Lord Wilton, for example. Egerton was a prime mover in the establishment in Manchester of musical festivals lasting several days. It would be rash to claim that Manchester originated these functions, but it certainly staged them on a new and lavish scale. The first, in 1777, was held to mark the opening of the concert hall; others followed in 1785, 1828, 1836 and 1844. It was at the 1836 festival that the celebrated mezzo-soprano Maria Malibran sang her last notes in public. She collapsed after the concert and died, aged twenty-eight, a few days later. Manchester was 'on the circuit' for visits by celebrities of the Malibran class (equivalent to a visit from Maria Callas at the height of her fame). Paganini played there in 1832. When Liszt was twenty-three he played twice in Manchester in 1825. Mendelssohn conducted *Elijah* there in April 1847. On his first visit to Manchester, Hallé heard the renowned soprano and tenor Grisi and Mario sing at a Gentlemen's Concert. He was also present when Chopin appeared as soloist at a Gentlemen's Concert on August 28, 1848, sandwiched between trios and cavatinas by Rossini. Chopin played his Andante and Scherzo, a Nocturne, Etudes and the Berceuse (the programme gave no further details) and he got a cool reception. Nevertheless no city's musical life can subsist solely on visiting celebrities, and resident connoisseurs such as Hermann Leo, who travelled abroad on business and heard the Parisian orchestra, realised how deficient Manchester's orchestra was. Hence his invitation to Hallé to 'take it in hand'.

A typical Gentlemen's Concert programme of 1838 consisted of a Haydn symphony, arias and duets by Rossini, Donizetti and Bellini, an Auber overture, and other miscellaneous pieces. Oratorios and extracts from Handel's works were regularly performed. The standard of soloists was high. Costa and Sir George Smart were guest

15

conductors on occasions, otherwise the concerts were led from the first violin desk by the Manchester musician C. A. Seymour. Hallé was joined in Manchester by his wife on September 6, 1848. His first concern was to find sufficient pupils to give him a living. Although Leo must have told him that the directorship of the Gentlemen's Concerts would eventually be his, nothing could be done for the 1848-49 season. Hallé's first regular contribution to Manchester's musical life, therefore, was a series of six concerts of chamber music given early in 1849 in the Royal Manchester Institution (now the City Art Gallery). The following winter 1849-50 he was joined in these by the violinist Ernst and from their partnership developed the Manchester Classical Chamber Concerts which continued until 1859 and at which Hallé and his colleagues performed programmes rich in interest.

Ernst and Hallé performed at a Gentlemen's Concert in August 1849. A few weeks later, Hallé was offered the post of conductor of the concerts. On October 21, 1849 he wrote (in French) to 'the directors of the Concert Hall' setting forth his conditions, which were accepted. These included power to 'hire and fire' players, money for better soloists, and more rehearsals. He also urged democratisation of the concerts by increasing the number of 'undress' concerts, to which a wider public had access. Some idea of Hallé's industry in his first year in a strange city can be gained from a notebook he kept which is now in the possession of Manchester City Librarian. He listed all the music he bought; he listed all the subscribers to his chamber concerts, how many tickets they bought and where they lived (thereby incidentally providing a fascinating and invaluable sidelight on Manchester life at that time: from it we know that Hermann Leo and Salis Schwabe, with whom Chopin stayed, were neighbours in George Street); he listed every move of his games of chess with Ernst and others; he listed the works of major composers performed in Manchester in the five years before his arrival; he kept detailed accounts of payments to musicians. There are many pages of English sentences copied in his beautiful handwriting from books and newspapers as an aid to his learning the language: the ink still looks as fresh as if it had been penned yesterday. It is a moving and eloquent document. So swiftly did Hallé master the language that within four years he was writing detailed, and still illuminating, programme-notes (with music examples) for his chamber concerts.

The first Gentlemen's Concert which Hallé conducted was on February 20, 1850. He began with an unspecified Haydn symphony and the programme included a Mozart symphony and extracts from Mozart's *Requiem.* On April 4 he conducted Beethoven's Fifth Symphony and on December 4 the 'Pastoral'. The 'Eroica', No.8 and No.4 followed during 1851 and he played the Third Concerto on August 6 of that year. During 1852 he conducted Mozart's 40th symphony and repeated Beethoven's Fifth. Otherwise the programmes remained a miscellany of shorter pieces, with much emphasis on operatic arias and duets. There seems no doubt that he felt trammelled by the size of the orchestra (forty players), for apart from *Harold in Italy* in 1855 he made no attempt to introduce Berlioz. The patience he had learned in Paris stood him in good stead in Manchester. The committee had not fulfilled some of the conditions under which he had accepted his post—not exactly a rare phenomenon in Mancunian musical affairs —as can be seen from his diary for 1855, and one is tempted to wonder how long he would have stayed if there had not been the opportunity for enlarging the orchestra which was occasioned by Manchester's munificence regarding the 1857 Art Treasures Exhibition, which lasted from May to the end of October. On September 8, 1857, for instance, he at last felt able to attempt Berlioz's *Carnaval Romain* overture, and a month later he conducted the first Manchester performance of Beethoven's Ninth Symphony. After this, to revert to the small orchestra and

17

the small Concert Hall would have been impossible, hence his courageous decision to strike out on his own and to take advantage of the existence since 1856 of the new large Free Trade Hall. (Later he had the foresight to realise the danger to his concerts of this being an all-purpose hall. He wanted a Hallé Hall exclusively for the concerts, a need that is still felt today). He continued to conduct the Gentlemen's Concerts but the programmes remained light and popular: all the weight went into his own series. Those first nine years in Manchester were crucial in other ways. He conducted a season of opera and he went seriously into the question of establishing an opera house and a conservatoire. In the first task he failed; the second took him forty years.

Hallé's was the first professional orchestra in Britain to rehearse and play together year after year, with personnel almost unchanged. Shaw wrote of the Hallé Band's 'rare combination of intimate knowledge of their repertory with unimpaired freshness of interest in it.' By his annual visits to Europe and by his friendships with such men as Brahms, Wagner, Joachim, Richter and Bülow, Hallé was also able to sustain a genuine international influence on Manchester's music and to attract distinguished foreign instrumentalists to live and teach in the city.

How soon Hallé's personality established itself in Manchester can be deduced from a letter written by Mrs Gaskell in 1852 in which she refers to having taken a subscription to 'Hallé's concerts'; to her, at any rate, that was what the Classical Chamber Concerts became in two years. No doubt the ladies of Manchester were attracted by this young man whose figure and appearance had reminded Schindler in 1840 of 'the princes of the Imperial House of Austria'! His personal charm was a telling factor in his success, but it was the courageous policy he followed for nearly fifty years that won him national esteem in his lifetime and earns the continuing respect of posterity. From 1858 to 1895 he revolutionised musical taste in a manner that smoothed the way for Henry Wood. Nevertheless the early Wood Promenade concerts of the 1890s employed audience-bait of a kind Hallé scorned even in 1858. He soon left behind ophicleide solos and pot-pourris of operatic favourites. By his third season he was giving complete concert performances of *The Magic Flute* and *Fidelio*. Gluck's *Iphigenia in Aulis* and *Armide* were performed in 1860 (another legacy of Berlioz's friendship). Hallé's season comprised twenty weekly concerts in Manchester with his own orchestra. He took it on regular tours, not only of Lancashire and Yorkshire but to Edinburgh, Bristol and London. Though it did not approach the arduous present-day schedule instituted by Barbirolli in 1943, Hallé's Hallé was busier than Harty's in the 1920s. Great names appeared as soloists at the concerts—the violinist Joachim, the mezzo-soprano Pauline Viardot, the pianist Hans von Bülow—but even more significant was the eagerness with which Hallé seized upon new works within a year or two of their first performances elsewhere: the symphonies of Brahms and Dvořák, Verdi's *Requiem*, the music of Wagner, Grieg, Saint-Saëns and Tchaikovsky and of many others besides, notably British composers such as Sullivan and Stanford. Moreover one performance rarely sufficed. Whether the critics and audience had liked it or not, an important new work would often be repeated in the next season. As a truly broad-minded pioneer and educator Hallé remains unequalled, in my submission, in the history of British musical life.

Of the man himself his autobiography reveals much by implication. His son's completion of it, fulsome as it may sometimes seem, is amply supported by other disinterested testimony. Hallé's players and pupils adored him; without risking loss of dignity and authority, he was free of all 'side'. He travelled with his orchestra, whiling away long train journeys playing cards for sixpence a game. There is a touching letter, written in 1888 by the Viennese violinist Ludwig Straus, who had been leader of the orchestra for sixteen years and wanted to retire, which tellingly illustrates his regard for Hallé: 'You asked me if I could not tell you verbally what I wished to write to you. I strove hard to do so when I drove home with you from the rehearsal, but it would not pass my lips . . .'

Sociability was something he had learned in Paris, and in England he continued to cultivate the company of writers and artists as well as of musicians. Manchester was not bereft of interesting and congenial inhabitants and in London he was the friend of the painters G. F. Watts and Frederick Leighton, of Robert Browning and John Ruskin. His social graces made him a sought-after guest at country-house parties but, notwithstanding his close associations with members of the Royal family, he was neither snob nor tuft-hunter. Probably after the death of his wife Désirée in April 1866 he was lonely, in spite of nine children, but it was not until twenty-two years later that he married again, taking as his wife Wilma Norman-Neruda, the great violinist, who was twenty years his junior and had appeared at a Gentlemen's Concert in May 1849 when she was ten (Seymour conducted). Theirs was a musical partnership unforgettable by those who heard it, but the letters Hallé wrote to his daughters when Wilma and he toured Australia and South Africa in the 1890s indicate also a close and comfortable domestic companionship.

It is Désirée of whom one would like to know more. We get a few glimpses of her in Mrs Gaskell's letters—kindnesses to Marianne Gaskell, to whom Hallé gave lessons; cancelling a ball after Prince Albert's death—and one letter of hers survives from 1848 in which she writes to her sister in New Orleans of her delight in the house Hallé had rented in Victoria Park[1] and of how happy she was in Manchester. But that is all. Of nine children, the eldest son, Charles, was an artist and a director of the Grosvenor Galleries, London. Gustave emigrated to Pietermaritzburg, South Africa, where his male descendants still live.

[1] No. 3 Addison Terrace. It still exists.

After Désirée's death, the eldest child, Marie, kept house in Manchester for her father. The second son, Frederick, died in 1879 in his early twenties and Clifford appeared as a tenor soloist at his father's concerts on two occasions in the 1880s. Three other children were Bernhard, Mathilde and Nora. The only two who married were Louise, to a Frenchman named Noufflard, and Gustave. Hallé returned regularly to Hagen to visit his mother who lived to a great age. Once, in a letter to Louise written when he was sixty-five, he gives expression for the first and only time to the poignancy of a lifetime of self-imposed exile, writing of his 'immense longing for the past'. His tastes in music show that he was a deeply emotional man, whatever the surface aspect. That he was a fighter, too, is evident from the tone of his letter in 1890 about the Edinburgh critics. As was inevitable with a man who remained in an influential position for over forty years, there were times when his popularity waned or when—sometimes for chauvinist reasons—his sway was challenged, but nothing serious developed from these mutterings.

There was never a thought that Hallé's concerts would be discontinued after his death. Three Manchester businessmen guaranteed them until the formation of the Hallé Concerts Society; and an approach was at once made to Hans Richter to take over the conductorship. Eventually he came and remained for twelve years. The Hallé conducting tradition is one of long service: Sir Hamilton Harty stayed for thirteen years and Sir John Barbirolli for twenty-seven. Each of these three great conductors would from their own experience have echoed Hallé's words on his seventieth birthday: 'One great point is that I can reckon, and have always reckoned, upon the goodwill and confidence of the Manchester public.' Of Charles Hallé it may truly be said that he has a living memorial—and one that he raised to himself.

Michael Kennedy

1

Early Years: Hagen and Darmstadt, 1819-36

With letters

I was born on April 11, 1819, at the moment when the church bells began to ring in Easter Morn, as my dear mother often told me in after years. Curiously enough, Easter Sunday fell every eleven years on April 11 until I was fifty-five years old, but will not do so again during my lifetime. Hagen, in Westphalia, where I saw the light, was then a little town with from 4,000 to 5,000 inhabitants. My father, Frederick Hallé, originally from Arolsen, in the principality of Waldeck, was organist of the principal church, and 'Musikdirektor', which means that he conducted the concerts, for, although the town was so small, there were concert societies there of no little importance. My father, besides, gave innumerable lessons in singing, as well as on almost every instrument. He had a charming tenor voice, and was a first-rate performer on the piano, the organ, the violin, and the flute. His activity was not restricted to Hagen alone, for when concerts were given in neighbouring towns, such as Iserlohn, Limburg, Dortmund, Schwelm, and others, he was generally invited to conduct them; and was known far and wide as a remarkable wit, many of his clever sayings being quoted for years. He was handsome, most winning in appearance, and nothing could equal the enthusiasm with which he cultivated his art, to which I owe the love, the adoration of music which has never left me during my long life. My dear mother, Caroline Hallé, *née* Brenschedt, came of an old Westphalian family. She was, when I could begin to appreciate her, one of the sweetest of God's children, and continued to be loved by all who knew her until her death at the ripe age of eighty-eight years. She also was a good musician, though not a professional one, and sang most charmingly with a sweet soprano voice. Often was I lulled to sleep, when a baby, by the duet-singing of my parents, but many years must have passed before I could understand the merit and beauty of it. I remained for upwards of eight years their only child, and feel sure that it has been given to few men or women to recollect so happy a childhood as mine was.

But this childhood had its troubles, although they were little felt by me. I have only learned in later years that my babyhood was most precarious—that I was a miserably weak child, and nobody, not even the doctor, thought I could live long. Although not actually ailing, I had to be brought up like a hothouse plant, was seldom taken into the open air, which at the period I speak of was mostly considered dangerous, and hardly ever admitted into a sickroom; and if I have outgrown that weakness, and falsified the prognostics of the doctor, I owe it probably to the tender care of a most loving mother. Through being kept constantly indoors, my life became different from that of other children; there was no romping for me in the playground or the garden, and my mother had to find occupation for me in the house. She first taught me to read when I was but three years old, and at the age of four I read as fluently as ever since. Together with the alphabet she taught me my notes, to amuse me, and as a natural consequence of the musical atmosphere in which we lived. Well do I remember a square book, bound in red morocco and containing music paper, in which she had written the notes with their names, and which altogether bore testimony to my progress, for all the little exercises and small pieces which I had to learn were written in this book, first by her, then by my father, when she handed me over to him. At that time it was most unusual to teach from a printed 'Pianoforte School'; the music master was expected in the case of beginners to compose exercises and short pieces during the lesson, and write them down in a book kept for that purpose by the pupil. Such was my book, which I treasured for forty years, until it was lost with my other luggage on a railway journey through Belgium. I have been told many a time by my parent teachers that I took to music with extraordinary eagerness, that it became my only joy, and that my progress was remarkably rapid. It must have been so, for the above-mentioned red book testified that at four years of age I played a little sonata, composed for me by my father, at one of the subscription concerts of the 'Concordia' Society.

About that time my constitution had become a little stronger, and my parents had hopes that I might live a few years longer. I was, therefore, less confined to the house, and now and then taken to a concert, which explains my appearance there as a most precocious soloist. To be taken to a concert, to listen to a symphony or an overture, was at that early age my greatest joy, and I may say that I grew up in music, and thought and dreamt of nothing else. And well was the life in Hagen calculated to foster this taste, for music seemed to be its chief occupation, just as it was in all the surrounding small towns with which I became acquainted in my boyhood. The number of good amateurs on various instruments was great; every house resounded with music; about ten subscription concerts were given every winter by the Concordia Society, the orchestra of which consisted of professionals and amateurs, about forty in number, and was conducted by my father. There was also a 'Gesang-Verein', which met once a week the whole year through, with the exception of two summer months, and of which my father had also the direction. With the

help of this society a few concerts were given in the summer
for the performance of some oratorios, a kind of small
festival to which the public flocked from all the neighbouring towns. To these societies I owe my earliest
acquaintance with most of the works of the greatest composers; for my progress upon the piano had been so rapid
that when I was still a child my father made me accompany at the meetings of the Gesang-Verein instead of
doing it himself. Thus I became thoroughly familiar with
'The Creation', 'The Seasons', 'The Mount of Olives', some
of Handel's and of Spohr's oratorios, with numerous other
works, at an age when they generally are but names to
other children. My functions at the subscription concerts
were of a different nature. I had taught myself the violin
up to a certain degree, in the hope of being enrolled as an
amateur second violin, but it so happened that the
gentleman who played the kettle-drums left the town, and
I, although seven years old, was considered so good a
timekeeper that my father promoted me to that important
and dangerous post. And for eight years did I hold it,
though not altogether to my credit; for although I found no
difficulty in coming in at the right time, perhaps on the
third beat after fifty-seven bars' rest, I could never accomplish a satisfactory roll, hard as I laboured at it. The
kettle-drum is not exactly an instrument suited to a
drawing-room, so I could get no practice, and I remember
even now how I envied and admired the drummers of any
military band that passed through our town, recognising
them by far my superiors.

My efforts at these concerts were, however, not confined
to the drums. Having once played a little solo on the piano
at the age of four, my kind friends,—and I believe the
whole town consisted of them—wanted to judge every year
of my progress, and I had, therefore, to play at least once
every season gradually more and more important pieces.
One of these appearances has left a lasting impression
upon my mind. I was then eight years old, and played the

variations by Ferdinand Ries on 'Am Rhein, am Rhein, da wachsen uns're Reben,' a stock piece at that time of a very brilliant character. Before the end of the piece, which I did not play from memory, I had to stop and tell my father that I could not see any more; there was a veil before my eyes. Our own doctor, who was one of the audience, came at once to look at me, and pronounced that I had the measles, a malady much dreaded at that time. So, instead of finishing the variations, I was carefully wrapped up, and carried home in my father's arms. I was long ill and confined to a room, the temperature of which was kept at summer heat, the fire never being allowed to go out. I was watched every night alternately by my father and my mother, and it so happened that one night when it was my father's turn, he had been overcome with fatigue and fallen asleep, and lo! when he awoke, the fire had burnt out. In his anxiety to light it again, there being no real firewood at hand, and the servant sleeping in another storey, he broke up his beloved flute, a yellow one, I remember—upon which I had heard him play many a solo by Tulau and other great flautists. The fire was relit, and he never regretted, or even alluded to, the sacrifice which his paternal love had induced him to make; but I cried bitterly over it when it came to my knowledge.

In course of time I was cured of the measles, but they left a very serious inflammation of the eyes, in consequence of which I was shut up for weeks in a dark room. There was a piano in it, and as soon as I felt strong enough I began to practise all my pieces from memory in the dark, having to feel for the keyboard, for there was not the slightest glimmer of light. I still remember how amused I was with certain variations by Abbé Gelinck (a very popular composer then, but now totally forgotten),[1] in which there were many rapid crossings of the hands, and how delighted I

---

[1] Usually known as Joseph Gelinek (1758-1825). He was one of the Viennese pianists whom Beethoven regarded as 'deadly enemies'. His variations and fantasies, of moderate difficulty, had a ready sale.

was when at last I could judge of the distances so as to hit the right notes. Illness forced me to try this experiment, but I should recommend it to many young players in good health, for it certainly improves the knowledge of the keyboard. After this temporary but severe illness music became again the all-absorbing interest of my young life, and by accident I gave evidence of having a good ear. Returning one day from a visit to a great-uncle who lived in the same town, and touching our piano, I said to my father that the pitch of my uncle's piano was a quarter of a tone lower than that of ours, and verification proved me to be correct, to the evident satisfaction of my parents. At the same time it became an amusement to them and to their friends to put me in a corner of the room, strike several notes together, sometimes the most incongruous and discordant ones, and make me name them, from the lowest upwards, which I invariably accomplished. This faculty has proved to have one drawback—viz. that the pitch of that period, a good half-tone lower than the present one, has remained so impressed on my brain, that when I now hear a piece of music for the first time, it seems to me in a higher key than it really is written in; I hear it in C when it is in B, and have to translate it, so to say. My friend Joachim shares this peculiarity with me, and it is now and then very perplexing.

At that time, when I was eight years old, school life had necessarily begun for me—for though far from robust, I was then in perfect health—and continued till the year 1835, when I had worked myself up to the second place in the highest class. But all my free hours were devoted to music, sometimes even those that ought not to have been free. The weekly meetings of the Gesang-Verein made me familiar with all the best choral works; the practice for the subscription concerts, with orchestral works, while my father had many quartet parties at our house, when I was allowed to turn the leaves, and made my first acquaintance with Haydn's quartets. Then my father often played with me pianoforte duets, the sonatas of Mozart, and arrangements of the symphonies by the great masters; also duets for piano and violin, as he was an excellent violinist, and my love for Mozart and Beethoven's violin sonatas dates from that early time. We also played trios with a friend of our family, Herr Elbers, a wealthy iron-merchant, a remarkable bass singer and good violoncellist, and how I enjoyed Beethoven's wonderful trio in B flat.[1] I cannot find words to express, nor can I describe the enthusiasm with which my father exclaimed: 'The whole of Beethoven is to be found in the Scherzo!' I must have played this trio before the year 1827, although I was only seven years old, for when I heard of Beethoven's death it seemed to me as if a god had departed, and I shed bitter tears. In addition to these musical experiences Herr Elbers invited me to spend one evening each week at his house for the sake of playing violoncello duets with him, and for many years these meetings were continued. They were a great pleasure to me, not the least part of the enjoyment consisting in the excellent supper which followed our musical exertions. He was an enthusiastic amateur, and I fully believe that we played every piano and violoncello duet, good, bad, or indifferent, composed up to that time. The five sonatas by Beethoven were repeated innumerable times and always with the same zest, but those by Hummel, Ferdinand Ries, even Reissiger and others were not neglected.[2]

In this manner my store of knowledge increased constantly. Music, heard by my inner ear, accompanied me at all times and during all my walks, and I created for myself a singular test by which to know if a piece of music was beautiful or not. There was a spot, a bench under a tree by the side of a very small water-fall, where I loved to sit and 'think music'. Then, going in my mind through a piece of

[1] The 'Archduke' Trio, opus 97. Composed 1811, published 1816.

[2] Johann Hummel (1778-1837) and Ferdinand Ries (1784–1838) were pianoforte pupils of Beethoven. Karl Reissiger (1798-1859) was a composer and conductor whose graceful and easy chamber works were popular for a time.

music such as Beethoven's 'Adelaide', or the Cavatina from 'Der Freyschütz', I could imagine that I heard it in the air surrounding me, that the whole of nature sang it, and then I knew that it was beautiful. Many pieces would not stand that test, however hard I tried, and those I rejected as indifferent.

During my childhood my father took his family every summer to his native town, Arolsen, on a visit to his elder brother, who inhabited the house in which he had been born. These visits were a delight to me, fond as I already was of travelling, and I looked forward to them for many months previous. The mode of travelling differed greatly from our present one, but was all the more enjoyable, especially to a young and impressionable mind. The journey would nowadays occupy about four hours, but at that time a sort of 'Vetturino', called *Hauderer* in German, was sent from Arolsen to fetch us, and the two amiable horses, driven by a coachman bearing the poetical, almost Wagnerian name of Friedewald, accomplished the distance in two days. On one of these visits, in August 1828, my father took me to Cassel, a drive of about four hours, in order to pay his respects to Spohr, who was then Kapellmeister there,[1] and at the same time to get his opinion as to my musical abilities. Spohr was at that time at the height of his reputation, not only as a violinist but as a composer. From our weekly practices at Hagen I knew his oratorios by heart, knew his concertos by having heard my father play them, and had been fascinated by his luscious melodies and wonderfully sweet harmonies and modulations. He was therefore one of my demi-gods, only a few degrees lower in my estimation than Beethoven, Mozart, and Haydn, with which revered names I always associated his. My excitement during the few minutes we had to wait for

---

[1] Louis Spohr (1784-1859) was well known as violinist, composer and conductor. He became Hofkapellmeister to the Elector of Hesse-Cassel in 1822, the post having been declined by Weber, who recommended Spohr. He maintained Cassel's position as a leading musical centre, especially for opera.

his appearance in his drawing-room was intense, and when his huge figure, looking twice its size through wearing a loose dressing-gown reaching to his feet, entered, I was awe-struck. He received us most kindly, and when I had quite recovered my breath he made me play to him, the result of which was that he insisted upon my giving a concert in Cassel, he himself undertaking all the arrangements, enrolling vocalists from the operatic troupe, actually two of the most celebrated singers of the time, the soprano, Mlle Heinefetter, and the tenor, Wild.[1] The concert took place in the first days of September, and created much interest, musical prodigies (I was nine years old) being then not so plentiful as they have since become. Of the programme, or rather my part in it, I ought to feel ashamed, for, in accordance with the fashion of the hour, it consisted of variations by Henri Herz and by Ries, but also, I am glad to add, of a rondo by Hummel, which, I hope, was more to my taste. As an executive display by a child it was much commended in the papers, some of which are still in my possession, and Spohr himself was pleased, so much so that, when I met him again after a lapse of more than twenty years, he began at once to speak of this concert, which I thought long forgotten.

I have dwelt upon this, my really first appearance before the public (for the concerts at Hagen were family affairs), at some length, because it was my only one during my childhood; my fond father, jubilant as he was at my success, saying to me on returning from the concert, 'My dear boy, once, and never again!' a resolve which he kept, and for which in later years I have felt profoundly grateful. The temptation to exploit me must have been very great, for we were not in affluent circumstances; but, although healthy then, I was far from strong, and it is doubtful if I could have

---

[1] Sabine Heinefetter was the eldest of three sisters who made names as singers. Spohr helped her early career. In 1843 Berlioz heard her in *Norma* and described her to Liszt as 'a real singer'. Franz Wild was the outstanding Austrian tenor of his day and was admired by Beethoven.

stood the wear and tear of the life of a musical prodigy, which consideration must have weighed heavily with him; and it is certain that my studies would have been arrested, my knowledge of music, instead of progressing, would have remained stationary for years, and my youthful enthusiasm for music might have been jeopardised.

After our return to Hagen from this momentous excursion, I plunged with renewed zest into my daily musical studies, and in addition to the piano and the violin began to play the organ. My father was organist at the principal church, and I had long been accustomed to accompany him every Sunday, and sit with him in the organ loft, watching his manipulation of the pedals and listening with delight to his improvisations. I now asked him, timidly at first, to allow me to replace him when simple chorales had to be accompanied. He granted this, sitting by my side to guard against any blunders which might have disturbed the congregation. I soon gained confidence, and after a few months I could often go alone to the church, and with the consent of the clergy replace him altogether. It was the custom then, and still may be, to accompany the Holy Communion by soft and appropriate music, always improvised, for, according to the varied number of communicants, it had to be of longer or shorter duration, and I well remember those minutes, and how hard I tried to make my improvisation impressive. It was a new branch of music that opened itself to me, to which I took most eagerly, and which gave me many new joys. At the same time my father presented me with Gottfried Weber's treatise of harmony and composition, one of the very best books on the subject ever written, which I devoured with eagerness.[1] For years I studied it diligently, and derived from it, not only great benefit, but also an inestimable amount of the purest pleasure.

There remains nothing to tell of my childhood except

---

[1] Gottfried Weber (1779-1839), a lawyer who founded Mannheim Conservatoire, wrote his *Versuch einer geordneten Theorie* between 1817 and 1821.

one incident, characteristic of the unconscious daring of a boy who does not appreciate the difficulties with which he has to contend. Hagen was visited every season by a travelling troupe of singers and actors, who during two months gave performances of operas, dramas, and comedies in the large ballroom of the principal hotel, where a stage was erected, there being no regular theatre in the town. About a month previous to their visit the director, Herr Conradi, came to form the orchestra by inviting all the best amateurs to take part in it along with a few professional players, and asking my father to conduct the performances, without any remuneration of course. The love of music was so great that he never met with a refusal, and my own progress upon the violin having been declared sufficient, I was enrolled as a second violin. Those were *fête* days for me, and I became intimately acquainted with many of the best operas by taking an active part in them. On one of these visits, when I was eleven years old, it chanced that after the first few weeks my father fell ill, thus threatening to bring the performances to a premature end. Herr Conradi was in despair, seeing which I, with a boy's confidence, offered to replace my father, was entrusted with the bâton, and remained at the conductor's desk to the end of the season. Among the operas which I conducted were 'Die Zauberflöte', 'Der Freyschütz', 'Die Schweitzer Familie' (by Weigl, forgotten now), 'Preciosa', 'Zampa', 'Fra Diavolo', 'Die Stumme von Portici' ('Masaniello'), 'Maurer und Schlosser' (by Auber), and others, and it will easily be believed that I felt my importance, and was not a little proud of it.[1] Nervousness I never felt, but sometimes I cried whilst conducting, when the scenes were very affecting, or when I was deeply moved by the beauty of the music. My acquaintance with an orchestra at so early an

---

[1] Hallé cannot be right in saying this happened when he was eleven, i.e. in 1830. *Zampa* did not have its first performance until 1831 and *Fra Diavolo* had only been produced in Paris in 1830.

age and under such circumstances has not been without
advantages to me in later years. The remembrance of these
performances, the first I ever witnessed, is still very vivid; I
enjoyed them thoroughly, and admired even the *mise-en-
scène*, which, of course, was of the most simple and primitive kind. Once the performance of 'Don Giovanni' was
enlivened by an amusing incident. In the first act, when the
Commendatore steps out of his house to chastise Don
Giovanni, and gets killed for his pains, instead of being
accompanied by servants with torches, he only carried a
candle which he let fall when drawing his sword. This
unfortunate candle kept burning on the ground in
dangerous proximity to the side scenes, but nobody perceived it except the dead Commendatore who, being the
director of the company and proprietor of all the scenery,
&c., tried in his anxiety by grunts and whispers to draw the
attention of somebody to the impending danger, and not
succeeding, deliberately sat up, put the candle out with a
wetted finger, and lay down again, dead as before. I did not
conduct that night, fortunately, for I am afraid I should
never have recovered my gravity sufficiently to bring that
act to its conclusion.

Few concert-givers visited our town, which offered but
small inducements to them; my opportunities for getting
acquainted with the outside musical world were therefore
very restricted. I remember, however, the visits of two
talented French children of little more than my own age,
Louis Lacombe and his sister, both pupils of the Conservatoire, and very clever pianists. The remarkable finish of
their execution impressed me greatly, and never did I
practise so diligently as after hearing them. Louis
Lacombe in after years made his mark in France both as a
pianist and composer, but I never met him again, although
as boys we were very intimate. The neighbourhood of
Hagen, especially Elberfeld, a flourishing town, was more
favoured, and my father went there on one occasion to hear
Paganini, about whom he raved for many months after-

33

wards. Madame Catalani,[1] the most celebrated singer of the time, also gave a concert there, which I remember from a description of her powers given to us by a non-musical friend who had made the journey from curiosity to hear her, and on his return, full of the most extraordinary enthusiasm, told my father: 'In one air she sang higher and higher, and when she could not get any higher, she still sang a little higher, and there *she did a roll!*' (meaning she made a shake).

So, until the age of fifteen, I continued this most happy life at home, steeped in music, my all-absorbing passion. Many happy hours I spent in putting the quartets by Haydn and Mozart, and some of the latter's concertos, into scores (full scores being then seldom attainable), gaining thus an insight into the working of the great masters I could not otherwise have obtained. My public appearances at the Concordia concerts continued annually, and became gradually more important. The A minor and A flat concertos by Hummel, the E flat and C sharp minor concertos by Ferdinand Ries, the D minor concerto by Kalkbrenner,[2] the C minor concerto by John Field, are some of those which I recollect having performed, as well as hosts of smaller pieces. Now and then I was allowed to play in one of the neighbouring small towns, but on the whole my father was against these exhibitions, for which, with great justice, he did not consider me ripe. He felt that it was now time to send me to some great masters for further study in harmony and the piano, and after long debate it was decided that I should first go to Darmstadt to study counterpoint with Rinck,[3] the celebrated organist, and then to Paris in order to take lessons from Kalkbrenner.

[1] Angelica Catalani, the highest paid soprano of her day. She was nearing the end of her career by the time of which Hallé writes.

[2] Friedrich Wilhelm Kalkbrenner (1788-1849), pianist and composer. He lived and taught in London from 1814 to 1823 and joined the pianoforte-making firm of Pleyel in Paris in 1824. He was a shrewd businessman.

[3] Johann Christian Rinck (1770-1846). His appointment at Darmstadt lasted from 1805 until his death.

So the chapter of my childhood was closed; a childhood so happy that even now it stands vividly before my eyes, and the recollection of its manifold enjoyments is one of my greatest pleasures. It was made still brighter by one of those friendships which, contracted in earliest youth, endure through life. The son of a schoolmaster, our nearest neighbour, one day older than myself, was my constant companion, and never can there have been a greater similarity of character, of taste, than between Cornelius Flüss and myself. We shared every joy, every grief, and, I may say, every dream. For we were dreamers both, as was manifested in many ways. Thus, when we were eleven years old, and got hold of Fenimore Cooper's exciting novel, 'The Last of the Mohicans', our imaginations were at once filled with a longing for wood-life, for wild adventure, and we plunged into a dense wood which crowned one of the hills near Hagen, sought out the most retired spot, forcing our way through brushwood, and there determined to build us a hut where we could play at Indians and think ourselves far away from any human beings. By cutting saplings and clearing a small piece of ground, we managed to construct a tiny hut, just large enough to creep into, covered it with branches and leaves, and there we often lay for hours, dreaming all kinds of dreams. It had been the work of weeks, for only spare hours could be devoted to it, but when completed we were not satisfied but must needs make a little ditch all around it with what implements we could stealthily bring to the spot, and then raise a tiny wall round our dwelling, which assumed the aspect of a miniature fortress, into which we retired with a most delicious feeling of isolation and safety from intruders, even though they were ever so many wild Indians. For two summers our hut was our joy and our secret, until one day we found it destroyed and an angry note put up by the proprietor of the wood to the effect that trespassers would be prosecuted and dealt with according to the utmost rigour of the law. So the stern reality shattered our dreams and taught us that God's nature was not free for boys to use, as we had fondly believed.

Another of our pleasures was to go out in the evening with a lantern to study the stars and the constellations; we did not, however, look at the skies by means of the lantern, but it enabled us to read the map, and in time we became great astronomers. Music was a further bond between us; his appreciation of the art being most keen, and his knowledge of its literature extensive. Cornelius in later years became one of the teachers at the Hochschule in Hagen, and remained my trusted friend till his death a few years ago, which seemed to deprive me anew of part of my beloved childhood. The world has changed so entirely during the last seventy years that children of the present day are no longer like the children of that past time. Where is the child to be found now that up to the age of eight or nine years will hold the firm belief that the gifts on Christmas morn are brought by an angel from heaven—'Christkindchen' in our homely German? Such was my belief, and that of all the children of my age. On Christmas Eve there stood the large empty table decked with white linen, in the drawing-room, ready to receive the gifts, and who could describe the feelings of confiding awe with which I knelt before the open window, praying the good angel to bring me nice gifts, and looking up to the stars wonderingly, and half afraid of seeing him descend? Then came the night, full of expectation, retarding sleep until very late, from which I was aroused at seven o'clock by my mother with the joyful words: 'Christkindchen ist hier gewesen' (Christ-child has been here). And lo! there stood the Christmas-tree, with its hundred tiny wax lights, its golden nuts and apples, in the middle of the table, covered now with toys and other small gifts, amongst which I always found a new piece of music, generally coveted long before. It was a happy day, and so deep and lasting has been its impression upon me, that wherever, and under whatever circumstances, I have spent Christmas Day, even when alone in Paris, I have had my Christmas-tree, got up by myself in the old fashion, sometimes under considerable difficulties. I was eight years old, I believe, when another boy, a little older than myself, told me that we owed the Christmas gifts to our parents, that they did not come from heaven. This gave me such a shock that I fell with both my fists upon the boy, pommelling him with all my might; but I got the worst of the battle, almost the only one I fought in my life, and came home crying to ask for confirmation of the dreadful tale. My dear mother had to give it, but did it in such a delicate way that, although I felt the mysterious poetry of that night was gone, my love for my parents was increased.

The summer in Hagen brought other delights when I was a little older. Placed in a lovely narrow valley on both sides of a small, clear river—the Volme—Hagen was surrounded by gardens, rich with fruit trees, strawberries, and other dainties. Through the narrow lanes formed by these gardens, and with the smell of the rich vegetation in our noses, my father walked every summer evening with me by his side, telling me stories of the great composers and anecdotes from his own musical life, thus filling me more and more with love for music. Great was my joy when now and then he took me on a fine afternoon as far as Limburg, a small town with a beautifully situated castle on the top of a hill, the residence of the Prince of Hohen-Limburg. This was a walk of about an hour, mostly through a forest of pine- and beech-wood covering two hills we had to pass. The goal of our promenade was an inn, Herr Polcher's, very primitive, but with a beautiful garden, a good assembly room, which generally, when my father's visit was expected, saw many of his friends assembled around a long table, the *réunions* being often graced by the presence of the good old prince himself, who was a great lover of music and the other fine arts, and fond of genial society. In spite of the large star that decked his breast, his princely dignity was soon forgotten in the banter of wit in which he good-

37

humouredly joined. I remember one amusing incident, the thought of which provokes my mirth even now. The whole company, prince included, sang in chorus a simple German ditty, 'Der La-la-la-la-Laudon rückt an' (Laudon advances), repeated innumerably; the fun consisting in the manner in which the leader (my father) started each repeat, which the whole company had to imitate, now giving it out in full stentorian voice, then in a whisper, now in sentimental adagio fashion, then in humorous dance rhythm, now standing, now sitting and turning their faces to the wall, every change being totally unexpected. In one variation my father jumped upon the chair, set one foot upon the table covered with bottles and glasses, a feat which the fat little prince had no slight trouble in imitating, and then the song had to be gone through without an audible sound, with motion of the lips only, the uplifted right hands marking the rhythm. At this moment one of the waiters entered with a fresh supply of bottles and glasses, and was so overcome by the extraordinary spectacle of so many guests having apparently gone suddenly mad that he let the bottles slip, and their crash and the stare on his astonished face changed the mute scene into one of boisterous laughter. After these good-natured follies came the enjoyable walk home through the still moonlight, the metallic notes of the innumerable frogs ('Unke') forming a concert, which often made our steps linger, and harmonised with my father's talk about music and musicians. Passing through the dark wood I crept close to him, my imagination peopling it with highway robbers, and found a sense of protection and comfort in the touch of his hand and the glow of his long pipe.

At that time the public force in Hagen consisted of one policeman and one night-watchman; it was fortunate, therefore, that robbers were not to be found in flesh and blood. The night-watchman, with his horn and long staff, was an object of mysterious interest to me, a shadowy form, only to be seen once every year, in the night from

December 31 to January 1, as I shall relate presently. But every evening I heard the sounds of his horn, blowing once at 10 o'clock, twice at 11, three times at midnight. What he did after that hour, if he added one blow at every hour or went to bed, I have never learnt. I was always happy to feel that some one was watching over me, and felt more comfortable in bed when I heard the horn and the simple ditty which the watchman sang every hour:

> Hört, ihr Leut, und lasst euch sagen,
> Die Glocke hat zehn [elf, zwölf] geschlagen:
> Bewahrt das Feuer und das Licht,
> Damit euch kein Schaden gebricht.[1]

Once in the year, on New Year's night, this performance was varied at 12 o'clock midnight. A chorus, principally of children, accompanied the watchman through the streets, and after the three notes of the horn, sang with him this verse;

> Das alte Jahr vergangen ist;
> Wir danken dir, Herr Jesu Christ,
> Dass du uns in so mancher Gefahr
> So gnädiglich behütet dies Jahr.[2]

The tune was one of the fine Lutheran chorales, but much embroidered. The first line in the original standing—

was sung—

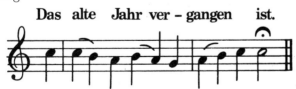

Das alte Jahr ver – gangen ist.

[1] 'Listen, people, and take heed. The clock has struck ten (eleven, twelve). Look well to your fire and light that no harm may come to you.'
[2] 'The old year is passed away. We thank thee, Lord Jesus Christ, for so mercifully preserving us in so many perils this year.'

The effect of the clear children's voices through the stillness of the night being heard faintly in the distance at first and gradually drawing nearer and nearer was over-powering to me, and made all my nerves tingle. I always insisted upon being led to the open window when the small singing crowd passed our house, and then I could admire the watchman with his lantern, look at him with deep-felt gratitude, and envy the children who were allowed to accompany and sing with him. Strange to say my recollection of those emotional nights is always associated with a clear starry sky, and pure white snow covering streets and houses, so that I sometimes wonder if the weather never was bad on December 31 in my early youth. It may have been so, but certainly very seldom, not often enough to tarnish their bright image. It was the custom of my father to sit up with his family into the New Year, drinking our health at the stroke of midnight in a glass of self-brewed punch (a custom which I have religiously preserved up to this day). It was the one exception to our early bed-going, and it was thus that I got a glimpse of the night-watchman, only to see him again after another year had elapsed.

As there was but one policeman and one night-watchman in Hagen, so there was also but one letter-carrier, a man beloved by all children on account of his great kindness to them. It was only in much later years, but when I was still a young man, that I heard the singular story of this man, and tried even, but unsuccessfully, to unravel the mystery connected with it. He was born at Aix-la-Chapelle in 1792, his parents being French emigrants; he was christened there, and his name entered in the register as Louis Chabot. He was confided to a nurse, his parents having to continue their flight, and for years he was amply provided for, until suddenly the supplies were stopped, and no further tidings were received from his family. He had no means of tracing them, and a life of misery began for him, through which he fought bravely, being at last stranded as the solitary postman at Hagen. The universal belief of all

who knew him and his story, a belief fully warranted by the
refinement of his manners and the dignity of his aristocratic bearing, was that he belonged to the great French
family of the Duc de Chabot-Latour. He himself believed
it, and in his humble circumstances lived so that a sudden
call to fortune and to an eminent position would have
found him quite fit for the change. The family of Chabot-
Latour was approached on his behalf, and on one occasion
a gentleman came from Paris to Hagen to inquire into the
circumstances, but apparently some link in the chain of
proof of his identity was missing, and Chabot—perhaps
Duke Chabot—died a postman, respected by the whole
community.

One more anecdote about Hagen and I shall leave the
dear place. Everybody knows that in Prussia there is a
State lottery, and in every town, big or small, there is a
collector, appointed to sell the tickets or 'Loose'. To the
collector in Hagen came a servant girl (in service in a
family of our acquaintance), and asked if she could buy
No. 23. He had not got it, but the girl seeming much in
earnest, he kindly promised to inquire if any of the collec-
tors in other towns had that particular ticket still to dispose
of, and he succeeded. The drawing took place some weeks
afterwards, and Hagen got into a state of feverish excitement when it became known that the girl had won one
of the big prizes, representing some thousands of pounds
sterling. She became of course the one object of interest in
the town, was 'interviewed' constantly, and when asked
how she could have fixed upon No. 23, she gave this simple
and lucid explanation: 'I dreamt one night No. 7, and a
second night I dreamt 7, and a third night 7 again, so I
thought 3 times 7 makes 23, and I bought that number!' So
much for the value of knowledge![1]

[1] 'The late Mr. Locker-Lampson relates in his *Confidences* that he heard this story from
Mr. Hallé – as he then was – and subsequently told it to the late Dean Stanley, whose
ignorance of arithmetic was notorious, and that the Dean, unable to see the joke,
observed, not without a shadow of dejection, "Ah, yes, I see, yes; I suppose three times
seven is *not* twenty-three".'—C.E.H.

In June, 1835, I left my beloved parents, and my dear native town, and travelled up the Rhine to Darmstadt, a two days' journey at that time. Rinck, a somewhat stout and elderly man, with a most benevolent countenance, received me most kindly, and helped me soon over the timidity with which I had approached him at first. Rinck was one of the most learned musicians in Germany, and his organ compositions, most of which I was familiar with, have remained models of their kind. The very next day we arranged for the beginning of my studies, but I was slightly taken aback when he fixed 6 o'clock in the morning as the hour of my lessons, and wondered also at the remark he made when appointing that early time: 'From five to six I compose'; the process of composing seeming to me scarcely compatible with fixed hours. But this habit may perhaps account for a certain dryness attached to most of his works. I worked very diligently during the year I remained with him, and apparently to his satisfaction.

It was, however, fortunate for me that I had studied harmony and counterpoint for years before, otherwise I might have profited little by Rinck's teaching. It was his custom, when correcting exercises, to say, 'I should have done it *so*,' never vouchsafing a reason for his corrections; the pupil, if advanced enough to understand and appreciate the improvement in Rinck's version, learned a great deal; if not, the teaching did not improve his knowledge. Besides working at strict counterpoint with my master, writing canons, fugues, &c., &c., my general musical studies were also largely directed by Gottfried Weber, to whom I had been introduced by Rinck. Weber, the author of one of the best works on harmony and composition, was not a professional musician, as he held a high position in the law; but there were few professional musicians who had his knowledge, his judgment, and his love for the art. He was no mean composer himself, having written Masses, cantatas, songs, and other works, and nobody could point out the beauties of the great composers' creations better than he did, or make one feel their power. Many were the works I had the privilege of studying with him, and delightful were the hours spent over them. It was he who made me first love and appreciate Cherubini, one of his favourites, with whose compositions I had, until then, been little acquainted. His mature mind also harboured the same enthusiasm for Beethoven which lived in my youthful soul, and nothing could be more interesting, or more instructive, than to hear him analyse some of the master's symphonies.

It was in Darmstadt also that I first heard a really fine orchestra—powerful and well trained, to which our homely orchestra in Hagen could not be compared. The then grand duke was a great lover of music, a musician himself, and under his watchful care Hofkapellmeister Mangold[1] had brought together a band equal to any of the best in Germany. To my great joy I was allowed to attend the rehearsals; and these were most numerous, taking place almost daily, and apparently merely for the pleasure of the practice. They seemed to be the only occupation of the members of the orchestra; in fact in quiet Darmstadt nobody appeared to have anything in particular to do, and nothing could exceed the stillness of its vast and regular streets. I remember up to the present day the deep impression which Beethoven's Eroica Symphony made upon me, especially the marvellous Funeral March. Sitting in a dark corner of the half-lighted theatre (the rehearsals took place on the stage), I was rapt in wonderment and trembling all over. There is in particular a long A flat for the oboe, about thirty-four bars before the close of the march, for which I always waited with perfect awe, and which made my flesh creep. The rehearsals of this one symphony were continued a full month, by the end of which I knew it by heart, not having missed a single one. During that month it was the all-absorbing topic of conversation amongst musicians,

[1] Wilhelm Mangold (1796-1875). Appointed 1825. An excellent violinist.

and the rehearsals, far from being shunned by the members of the orchestra, as is so often the case, were expected with impatience.

The studies with Rinck and Weber, and the equally important study of the works of the best composers, either by hearing them in Darmstadt or in Frankfort or by reading them, made me neglect the piano to a certain extent; nevertheless I had many opportunities of playing in private circles, and if I did not make any progress as a pianist during the year in Darmstadt, I promised myself to work all the harder in Paris, where the study of the piano would not be interfered with by anything, and would be my sole object.

Letters from Darmstadt
Translated from the German[1]

[To his parents, July 6, 1836]

. . . What pleases me best about Rinck is that he insists so much upon practical exercises, and thinks very little of mere theory; also, that he does not cling too much to the old rules: thus, he only forbids consecutive fifths when two greater fifths follow each other, one greater and one smaller fifth he willingly allows—that is to say, in several-part writing, for in two-parts it always sounds badly—his chief motto is: Lay no fetters upon Art. . . during a walk Rinck asked me what my plans were after leaving here (N.B.—*he has now given me the fullest assurance that it will not be necessary for me to remain six months with him*). I told him our intention was that I should go to Paris from here; of this he highly approved, and promised to give me letters of introduction to *Cherubini* and *Meyerbeer*, whom he knows very well, the latter especially, and he will strongly recommend me to both; you will rejoice at this as much as I; a letter from Rinck to *these*

[1] This and other translations are taken from *Life and Letters of Sir Charles Hallé*, 1896. Throughout the present edition omitted passages within letters are indicated by three dots.

two would be of the greatest use to me, for Cherubini is the Director of the Conservatoire, and you know how great the fame of Meyerbeer is just now in Paris. He will also give me letters to Ferdinand Hiller and other celebrated composers, whose names I cannot at present remember.

. . . The first letter I delivered at Darmstadt was the one to Fräulein Mangold. The first reception was so dry and formal that I went home quite out of humour, but yesterday I was invited to a large party, where I enjoyed myself greatly. I made the acquaintance of Kapellmeister Mangold, of Concertmeister Mangold (an excellent violoncellist), and of two other Mangolds, one of them a very good violinist, and who, according to Rinck, must be quite a genius; there were several other gentlemen and many ladies. I had to play several times, and the two Mangolds and I have agreed often to play duets and trios together. The Kapellmeister, a very nice man, at once made the proposal, if I wished to attend the rehearsals of the orchestra, that I should go any morning at 10 o'clock to the Court Theatre. I went this morning, and my joy was quite indescribable. The orchestra consists of more than sixty members; they play like angels, I have never heard anything like it, and I must describe it more closely another time. To-day they played Beethoven's 'Eroica Symphony'—that is, indeed, a mighty composition—at times an icy cold shiver ran through me, but more of this later. . . .

Your loving son

Carl Hallé

[To his parents, July 23, 1836]

. . . I will begin by telling you how I was received by Gottfried Weber. A few days after my arrival I went to his house at eleven o'clock in the morning, and was fortunate enough to find him; when I had given him Schott's letter, he kindly bade me sit down; whilst he was reading it I had a good look at him. Weber is a tall, strong-looking man, with a round, full face, very yellow and much scarred. He wore a large dressing-gown, a voluminous cravat tied loosely round his neck, and a white night-cap, which he never removed, as he has a perfectly bald head (so, at least, it seemed to me). When he had read the letter, he welcomed me once more, and asked if I had begun my lessons with Rinck. I told him I had only had one so far, and then I had to relate all that Rinck had made me do, with which he was much satisfied, and praised him for always proceeding to practise at once. He then asked if I had already composed much. I said no; not much as yet. He told me that was not right; that one ought to compose a great deal from the first, and could study the so-called thorough-bass style at any time. At the words, 'so-called thorough-bass style,' the fellow put on so sublime a sneer, that his face must have looked just so whilst he was writing his abuse of the thorough-bass style in his theory of music. After a little further talk, he asked what I intended to do after leaving Darmstadt, and when I told him of my plan of going to Paris, he said he envied me. He invited me to come and see him often, but so far I have not been able to go again, and he also has been out of town. On Monday or Tuesday I shall certainly go and try and sound him whether he would give me a letter for Kalkbrenner, should Rinck not do so. I go to the Mangolds nearly every day. Carl Mangold, the violinist, and I have become intimate friends, and as often as we are together, we play duets; sometimes, with the addition of an excellent violoncellist from the Court apothecary, no! I mean from the Court orchestra, we play trios. I have thus got acquainted with many works hitherto unknown to me; for instance, I now know *all* Beethoven's sonatas for piano and violin, nearly all his trios, further, six trios by Reicha, and three trios by Prince Ferdinand of Prussia, which are very fine, and many other things besides. The 'cellist, Wilhelm Mangold, who has no piano at his rooms, but lives just opposite to me, often comes over with his bass tucked under his arm, and then we play double sonatas by Beethoven, Onslow, &c., to our hearts' content.

That under these conditions I feel quite in my element you will easily believe. Next week we shall also play quartets and quintets with pianoforte. On August 25 there is to be a great concert in aid of the Beethoven monument, which will take place in the theatre, and probably last two days.

The Grand Ducal Kapelle is now in full rehearsal; none but Beethoven's compositions are to be performed. As often as I can find time, I go in the morning to the theatre to hear the rehearsal. I have now heard the 'Eroica' and the delicious Pastoral symphonies so often that I know them almost by heart; still, I go again and again, as I can never hear them enough. Now they are studying the great symphony with chorus, which I am most curious to hear. Such precision I had never heard in an orchestra, and had never thought it possible that such fine *nuances* could be obtained from such a numerous body; even the smallest indications were observed. They succeeded admirably in those crescendos which suddenly pass into *piano*, which are found almost exclusively in Beethoven's works. To be sure, Mangold, the conductor, takes enormous pains, one may say that he is indefatigable; for instance, at several rehearsals, before taking the whole orchestra together, he takes the first violins with only two of the other stringed instruments, and thoroughly drums their part into the first violinists, then he does the same with the second violins, with the violas, and with the 'cellos and five double-basses; thereby the quartet gets so perfect that you do not hear a single false note. The *pizzicato* is also something quite exquisite. In Beethoven's 'Eroica' symphony there is a great deal of *pizzicato*, even whole runs in unison, but I was never able to detect one instrument arriving a little late; each time it came like a spark, and the effect was most extraordinary.

I had almost forgotten one thing, about which Carl Mangold gives me no peace, and which I have promised to write to you about. He goes in the middle of September to Vienna, and absolutely insists upon my going with him there instead of to Paris. He says there are as many pianists in Vienna as at Paris, and that one has more opportunities of hearing great works, oratorios especially, than in Paris (this I doubt). Further, that it would be good for us both to study composition again (he is going to take lessons from Seyfried, especially in free style, although he has studied harmony for years with his brother the Kapellmeister, who had worked three years under Cherubini, and, either before or after, with Spontini; he is exceedingly industrious, for a whole year composed a fugue every day, and has acquired such facility that he can produce a beautiful fugue in a quarter of an hour). However agreeable this would be, and however much I should like to continue my intercourse with one whose devotion, heart and soul, to music is greater than I ever met with before, and, indeed, passes all belief, I still prefer to go

47

to Paris, and believe it would be more useful to me. Therefore, dear father, I beg you, in your next letter, to put forward some good reasons why you prefer that I should go to Paris, which I can read to him, as I have always told him the decision rested entirely with you, and have never shown myself averse from the project; for when we are together I could wish to stay together always, and still, I would sooner go to Paris. Moreover, the cholera is at Vienna, certainly a good reason for you, dear mother, to insist upon my not going there. . .

Darmstadt: September 8, 1836

My dearest Parents— . . . Your letters are all safely to hand. I found them at midnight on the 28th of last month, on my return home after a brilliant tea and supper party. I opened them at once, but delayed reading them until the next morning, my mind, head, and inside being still too replete with the varied pleasures of the evening. . . . I am studying hard, and for the past few weeks have worked at nothing but fugues, at first three-part, and now four-part fugues, and shall do nothing else whilst I am here. Rinck's teaching pleases me less and less, but Rinck himself I like better and better. I practise harder and harder, and have bought some new music—for instance, Kalkbrenner's 'Effusio Musica', undisputably his best work, and Chopin's Variations on 'La ci darem' from 'Don Giovanni'. This is so dreadfully difficult, that I have to study it bar by bar, but I think that when I have overcome the difficulties (which will probably take a long time) I shall find it to be one of the most delightful works I know. These variations are far from being considered among his most difficult works, from which God preserve us!

My life here is exceedingly pleasant; it is quite a new existence for me. The most delightful hours are those I spend in the house of Mr. von Plöennies (*Medizinalrath*). One meets the whole artist-world of Darmstadt there: painters, musicians, poets—all artists are welcome. I have made many interesting acquaintances there, first among them Ed. Duller the writer, who lives here; also a Doctor of Philosophy named Kringel, quite a young man, whom I shall meet again this winter in Paris. I was introduced by Kapellmeister Mangold, and since then have been invited several times a week to grand tea and other parties. A striking elegance reigns in the house, which is a little embarrassing at first, but one's shyness is soon dissipated by the cheerful and easy tone which one hardly expects to find allied with such magnificence. The central point towards which all converges is certainly Mrs. von Plöennies. She is a distinguished poetess, and moreover a very handsome and most amiable lady, who enlivens the whole conversation. At these parties the entertainment is most varied; either Duller or Mrs. von Plöennies reads one of their latest compositions, then there is music. I have had to play each time, on a very find grand piano, only a little hard to play on; duets and quartets are sung, and so on; all this to a flowing accompaniment of wine and punch, whilst the palate is also most delicately catered for. I always return home very well pleased from one of these parties. You can therefore believe that I am sorry to be going away so soon; but as regards my studies I am glad, for I shall have time in Paris to chew the cud of all I have devoured so quickly in these three months with Rinck. . . .

Now, dearest parents, *lebt recht wohl.* . . . Your ever loving

Carl

Darmstadt: September 23, 1836
Highly honoured Herr Elbers—

. . . At present, before leaving Darmstadt, I can only thank you for your kind letter and the good advice and welcome news that it contained, as well, most especially, for the letters of introduction you were good enough to send. To write you a long letter just now would be impossible, for I am surrounded by a most confused chaos (but not one out of Haydn's 'Creation') as I am busy packing. . . .

I can only, therefore, tell you briefly that the three months I have spent here have passed very happily. I have made many and very pleasant acquaintances, especially with several members of the most excellent Court Orchestra. One of them, a first-rate violoncellist called Mangold, I have often played duets with, thus carrying on what I had begun with you at Hagen. The Court Orchestra, which contains from sixty to seventy musicians, is rather given to be idle during the summer months, but, luckily for me, since my arrival there have been rehearsals every morning from 10 to 1 o'clock for two concerts in aid of the

49

Beethoven monument, which have just lately taken place. I have there heard Beethoven's masterpieces, his symphonies, the second act of 'Fidelio', and his fantasia for pianoforte, orchestra, solos, and chorus, given in the highest perfection. You will believe that it was in the highest perfection when I tell you that the *Kapelle*, certainly one of the best in Germany, has, for a quarter of a year, studied these works regularly three hours a day.

I now clearly see that Beethoven's works are not, as it is usually considered, only capable of being appreciated by connoisseurs, but, when thus interpreted, even the musically uneducated who have minds in the least susceptible, must be impressed by them as by every work of the highest art.

I should be glad to speak with you more minutely about those performances, but I feel my incapacity to describe these sublime works of art with my pen, or to give the faintest idea of the impression that they made upon me. Therefore I shall remain silent, and reserve all I could possibly say for future verbal intercourse with you.

As to Rinck's method of teaching, I shall write to you fully when I am quietly settled in Paris. For himself personally, my worthy and never-to-be-forgotten master and friend, he is easily to be described. If you imagine the greatest goodness of heart shining through every feature and every act, combined with the greatest candour and simplicity of manner, and therewith, even in old age, an undimmed and glowing love of his art, you have his perfect picture. Certainly, seldom or never was a master more beloved by all his pupils. I have to thank him specially for introducing me to the artist world of Paris, through letters to Meyerbeer, Mainzer, Hiller, Schlesinger, and others. I now stand at the point for which I have been longing, when I shall come into contact with such celebrated members of the world of art. I am going to Paris with the highest expectations. . . .
Sometimes remember in the far distance your devoted and obliged friend,

Carl Hallé

2

Arrival in Paris, 1836

With letters

I left Darmstadt and my dear old master with sincere regret in the autumn of 1836, travelling by 'diligence' *via* Metz and Chalons, sleeping at each place by order of the doctor, for I was even then not very robust, and such a journey was at the time a formidable undertaking. A great disappointment awaited me after having crossed the French frontier and finding myself in the interior of the huge 'diligence' with four Frenchmen. At school I had been considered a very fair French scholar, reading and even speaking the language with a certain amount of fluency; great, therefore, was my astonishment when I did not understand a word of the conversation of my fellow-travellers, although I was all attention, and I arrived in Paris very crestfallen. It took a long time before my ear got accustomed to the unfamiliar sound, but then my former studies proved of great advantage. I may relate here that when two years later I paid a visit to Hagen and met my old teacher of French he addressed me joyfully in what he believed to be that language, but I no longer understood *him*, and he left me fully convinced that I had forgotten all he had taught me.

Arrived in Paris, and settled in a small German hotel in the Rue Vivienne, I began after a few days to deliver the letters of introduction I had brought with me, one of my first visits being to Kalkbrenner. Kalkbrenner and Hummel were at that time considered the greatest pianists, and even Chopin had come to Paris a few years before to learn from Kalkbrenner. I therefore approached him with considerable trepidation, and great was my disappointment when he told me that he no longer took pupils.[1] He, however, kindly invited me to play something, to which he listened carefully, and then made some unpleasant remarks and advised me to take lessons from one of his pupils. As I was about to leave him he offered to play for me, saying that it might prove useful to me to hear him. I accepted eagerly and was full of expectation, when he sat down and played a new piece of his composition, entitled 'Le Fou', one of the most *reasonable* and dullest pieces ever perpetrated. I admired the elegance and neatness of his scales and legato playing, but was not otherwise struck by his performance, having expected more, and wondering at some wrong notes which I had detected.

I did not at once follow his advice with regard to the teacher he had recommended, and two or three days later I received an invitation to dinner from the banker Mallet, to whom an uncle of mine, Harkort of Leipzig, had recommended me, and found myself sitting beside Chopin. The same evening I heard him play, and was fascinated beyond expression. It seemed to me as if I had got into another world, and all thought of Kalkbrenner was driven out of my mind. I sat entranced, filled with wonderment, and if the room had suddenly been peopled with fairies, I should not have been astonished. The marvellous charm, the poetry and originality, the perfect freedom and absolute lucidity of Chopin's playing at that time cannot be described. It was perfection in every sense. He seemed to be pleased with the evident impression he had produced, for I could only stammer a few broken words of admiration, and he played again and again, each time revealing new beauties, until I could have dropped on my knees to worship

[1] Compare the ensuing with Hallé's letters written at the time (see pages 63–68).

him. I returned home in a state of complete bewilderment, and it was only the next day that I began to realise what was before me—how much study and hard work, in order to get that technical command over the keyboard, without which I knew now that no good result could be achieved. Strange to say, the idea of taking lessons did not occur to me then; I felt that what I had to do could be done without a master; lessons of style might be more useful later on. I shut myself up and practised twelve hours and more a day, until one day my left hand was swollen to about twice its usual size, causing me considerable anxiety. For some months I hardly ever left my rooms, and only when I received invitations to houses where I knew I should meet, and perhaps hear, Chopin. There were not many of them in Paris, for Chopin, impelled by growing weakness, began even then to lead a very retired life. He used still to visit principally Count de Perthuis, the banker August Leo, Mallet, and a few other houses. Fortunately for me I had been introduced by letters to the above three gentlemen, and enjoyed the privilege of being invited to their '*réunions intimes*', when Chopin, who avoided large parties, was to be present. With greater familiarity my admiration increased, for I learned to appreciate what before had principally dazzled me. In personal appearance he was also most striking, his clear-cut features, diaphanous complexion, beautiful brown waving hair, the fragility of his frame, his aristocratic bearing, and his princelike manners, singling him out, and making one feel the presence of a superior man. Meeting often, we came into closer contact, and although at that time I never exhibited what small powers I might possess as a pianist, he knew me as an ardent student, and divined that I not merely admired but understood him. With time our acquaintance developed into real friendship, which I am happy to say remained undisturbed until the end of his too short life.

From the year 1836 to 1848, a period during which he

created many of his most remarkable works, it was my good fortune to hear him play them successively as they appeared, and each seemed a new revelation. It is impossible at the present day, when Chopin's music has become the property of every schoolgirl, when there is hardly a concert-programme without his name, to realise the impression which these works produced upon musicians when they first appeared, and especially when they were played by himself. I can confidently assert that nobody has ever been able to reproduce them as they sounded under his magical fingers. In listening to him you lost all power of analysis; you did not for a moment think how perfect was his execution of this or that difficulty; you listened, as it were, to the improvisation of a poem and were under the charm as long as it lasted. A remarkable feature of his playing was the entire freedom with which he treated the rhythm, but which appeared so natural that for years it had never struck me. It must have been in 1845 or 1846 that I once ventured to observe to him that most of his mazurkas (those dainty jewels), when played by himself, appeared to be written, not in 3-4, but in 4-4 time, the result of his dwelling so much longer on the first note in the bar. He denied it strenuously, until I made him play one of them and counted audibly four in the bar, which fitted perfectly. Then he laughed and explained that it was the national character of the dance which created the oddity. The more remarkable fact was that you received the impression of a 3-4 rhythm whilst listening to common time. Of course this was not the case with every mazurka, but with many. I understood later how ill-advised I had been to make that observation to him and how well disposed towards me he must have been to have taken it with such good humour, for a similar remark made by Meyerbeer, perhaps in a somewhat supercilious manner, on another occasion, led to a serious quarrel, and I believe Chopin never forgave him. Any deliberate misreading of his compositions he resented sharply. I remember how, on one occasion, in his gentle way he laid his hand upon my shoulder, saying how unhappy he felt, because he had heard his 'Grande Polonaise', in A flat, *jouée vite!* thereby destroying all the grandeur, the majesty, of this noble inspiration. Poor Chopin must be rolling round and round in his grave nowadays, for this misreading has unfortunately become the fashion.

I may as well continue to speak about Chopin here and take up the thread of my narrative later on, all the more as it will fill little space. His public appearances were few and far between, and consisted in concerts given in the 'Salon Pleyel', when he produced his newest compositions, the programme opening, I think, invariably with Mozart's Trio in E major, the only work by another composer which I ever heard him play. He was so entirely identified with his own music that it occurred to no one to inquire or even to wish to know how he would play, say, Beethoven's sonatas. If he was well acquainted with them remains a moot point. One day, long after I had emerged from my retirement and achieved some notoriety as a pianist, I played at his request, in his own room, the sonata in E flat, Op. 30, No. 3, and after the finale he said that it was the first time he had liked it, that it had always appeared to him very vulgar. I felt flattered, but was much struck by the oddity of the remark. In another direction, he did not admire Mendelssohn's 'Lieder ohne Worte', with the exception of the first of the first book, which he called a song of the purest virginal beauty. When one reflects on the wonderful originality of his genius, the striking difference of his works from any written before him, without making comparison as to their respective worth, one feels it natural that he should have lived in his own world, and that other music, even the very greatest, did not touch all his sympathies.

When I first knew him he was still a charming companion, gay and full of life; a few years later his bodily decline began; he grew weaker and weaker, to such a degree, that when we dined together at Leo's or at other friends' houses, he had to be carried upstairs, even to the first floor. His spirits and his mental energy remained, nevertheless, unimpaired, a proof of which he gave one evening, when, after having written his sonata for piano and violoncello, he invited a small circle of friends to hear it played by himself and Franchomme.[1] On our arrival we found him hardly able to move, bent like a half opened pen-knife, and evidently in great pain. We entreated him to postpone the performance, but he would not hear of it; soon he sat down to the piano, and as he warmed to his work, his body gradually resumed its normal position, the spirit having mastered the flesh. In spite of his declining physical strength, the charm of his playing remained as great as ever, some of the new readings he was compelled to adopt having a peculiar interest. Thus at the last public concert he gave in Paris, at the end of the year 1847 or the beginning of 1848,[2] he played the latter part of his 'Barcarolle', from the point where it demands the utmost energy, in the most opposite style, pianissimo, but with such wonderful *nuances,* that one remained in doubt if this new reading were not preferable to the accustomed one. Nobody but Chopin could have accomplished such a feat. The last time I saw him was in England; he had come to London a few weeks after my arrival there in 1848, and I had the privilege and the happiness to hear him several times at Mrs. Sartoris's and Henry F. Chorley's houses. The admiration which he elicited knew no bounds; there we heard for the first time the beautiful valses, Op. 62, recently composed and published, which since have become the most popular of his smaller pieces. I had the pleasure afterwards to welcome him to Manchester, where he played at one of the concerts of the society called the

---

[1] Auguste Joseph Franchomme (1808-84), an outstanding cellist.

[2] On February 16, 1848. Besides pianoforte solos, he played part of his own cello sonata with Franchomme and Mozart's Trio in G. (K.496) with Franchomme and the violinist Delphin Alard (who played Beethoven's concerto, with Hallé conducting, in Manchester on May 27, 1850).

Gentlemen's Concerts in the month of August.[1] It was then painfully evident that his end was drawing near; a year later he was no more.

To return to my own experiences in 1836, I have to relate that a few days after having made the acquaintance of Chopin, I heard Liszt for the first time at one of his concerts, and went home with a feeling of thorough dejection. Such marvels of executive skill and power I could never have imagined. He was a giant, and Rubinstein[2] spoke the truth when, at the time when his own triumphs were greatest, he said that, in comparison with Liszt, all other pianists were children. Chopin carried you with him into a dreamland, in which you would have liked to dwell for ever; Liszt was all sunshine and dazzling splendour, subjugating his hearers with a power that none could withstand. For him there were no difficulties of execution, the most incredible seeming child's play under his fingers. One of the transcendent merits of his playing was the crystal-like clearness which never failed for a moment even in the most complicated and, to anybody else, impossible passages; it was as if he had photographed them in their minutest detail upon the ear of his listener. The power he drew from his instrument was such as I have never heard since, but never harsh, never suggesting 'thumping'. His daring was as extraordinary as his talent. At an orchestral concert given by him and conducted by Berlioz, the 'March au Supplice', from the latter's 'Symphonie Fantastique', that most gorgeously instrumented piece, was performed, at the conclusion of which Liszt sat down and played his own arrangement, for the piano alone, of the same movement, with an effect even surpassing that of the full orchestra, and creating an indescribable *furore*. The feat had been duly announced in the programme beforehand, a proof of his indomitable courage.

[1] August 28, 1848. The recital was coolly received

[2] Anton Rubinstein (1830-94), regarded by many of his contemporaries as Liszt's only rival in formidable virtuosity.

If, before his marvellous execution, one had only to bow in admiration, there were some peculiarities of style, or rather of musicianship, which could not be approved. I was very young and most impressionable, but still his tacking on the finale of the C sharp minor sonata (Beethoven's) to the variations of the one in A flat, Op. 26, gave me a shock, in spite of the perfection with which both movements were played. Another example: he was fond at that time of playing in public his arrangement for piano of the 'Scherzo', 'The Storm', and the finale from Beethoven's 'Pastoral Symphony'; 'The Storm' was simply magnificent, and no orchestra could produce a more telling or effective tempest. The peculiarity, the oddity, of the performance, consisted in his playing the first eight bars of the 'Scherzo' rather quicker than they are usually taken, and the following eight bars, the B major phrase, in a slow andante time; 'ce sont les vieux', he said to me on one occasion. It may serve to characterise the state of musical knowledge in Paris, at the time I speak of, when I state that at a concert given by Liszt in 1837, in the Salle Erard, the B flat Trio by Beethoven, which stood at the commencement of the programme, and Mayseder's Trio in A flat, which was to begin the second part, were transposed for some reason or other, without the fact being announced to the public. The consequence was that Mayseder's Trio, passing for Beethoven, was received with acclamation, and Beethoven's very coldly, the newspapers also eulogising the first and criticising the length and *dryness* of the other severely. Of the *man* Liszt I shall have now and then something to say when I arrive at the time of our more intimate acquaintance.

With Thalberg[1] there came a new sensation in the same year. Totally unlike in style to either Chopin or Liszt, he was admirable and unimpeachable in his own way. His

---

[1] Sigismond Thalberg (1812-71), pupil of Kalkbrenner. Often compared to Liszt from about the time of Hallé's arrival in Paris, he made a deep impression on both Mendelssohn and Schumann.

performances were wonderfully finished and accurate, giving the impression that a wrong note was an impossibility. His tone was round and beautiful, the clearness of his passage-playing crystal-like, and he had brought to the utmost perfection the method, identified with his name, of making a melody stand out distinctly through a maze of brilliant passages. He did not appeal to the emotions, except those of wonder, for his playing was statuesque; cold, but beautiful and so masterly that it was said of him with reason he would play with the same care and finish if roused out of the deepest sleep in the middle of the night. He created a great sensation in Paris, and became the idol of the public, principally, perhaps, because it was felt that he could be imitated, even successfully, which with Chopin and Liszt was out of the question.

The hearing of Liszt and Thalberg put Kalkbrenner's advice still more in the shade. I went on listening to the three mighty heroes as often as I had an opportunity and relentlessly pursuing my studies by myself. By the help of some influential introductions I had brought with me, I made by degrees interesting acquaintances. It was probably on account of my youth, and my great enthusiasm for music, that I was at once treated with great kindness by men at the zenith of their fame and much older than myself. This was the case with Meyerbeer, Halévy, Liszt, and others, to whose nearer acquaintance I was helped through the then all powerful music-publisher, Maurice Schlesinger. The Parisian artistic and literary society, at that time, was so constituted that to know a few men of mark was to know them all, and certainly more by luck than by any merit, I soon found myself at home in circles of which I had read and dreamed, but which I had not hoped to enter. Gradually I had then to throw off my reserve and to play when I was asked, confining myself to excerpts from Beethoven and a few other composers. I met with success and encouragement, but for three years I resisted all attempts to make me appear in public, for which I did not feel myself ripe. During this time of labour I was visited one day, only a few months after my arrival, by a gentleman, Monsieur Guibert, a rich 'agent-de-change', who had heard of me, and made me the following proposal. He had two sons, ten and twelve years of age, was extremely fond of music, his wife and only brother equally so, and he wished to form the taste of his boys and make them thoroughly acquainted with the best compositions, for which purpose he asked me to devote one evening every week to himself and his family, and play for them whatever I liked and as much as I liked. It reminded me of the evenings with Herr Elbers; and M. Guibert adding a very handsome pecuniary inducement to his proposal, we soon agreed, and from that time for years I dined every Thursday at his table and revelled in music for hours afterwards. No strangers were admitted, and it was a delight to me to expound and make them feel the beauties of the various works we went through. Of course the sonatas of Beethoven were chiefly and diligently studied, but Mozart, Haydn, Bach, Weber, Dussek, Hummel, Clementi, and others were not neglected. I even played the arrangements of Beethoven's, Mozart's, and Haydn's symphonies; in fact, there was hardly anything in the whole range of music capable of being rendered on the piano with which I did not get familiar by familiarising my friends with it. These *séances*, repeated so constantly—for we only allowed a break of a few months in the summer—were of immense advantage to myself, for there were many pieces I might have neglected but for the desire to increase our *répertoire* to the utmost.

I owe them also one great joy which alone would have made them for ever worthy of my remembrance. It was in 1838 that M. Guibert asked if for once I would allow him to admit a friend, a sincere lover of music, to be present on one of our evenings. The request being readily granted, the friend came on the following Thursday, and turned out to be Salvator Cherubini, the eldest son of one of my idols, the great composer. Overjoyed as I was, my rapture became indescribable when a few days later M. Salvator called upon me with a message from his father, to the effect that he wished to make my acquaintance and hoped I would sometimes spend a Sunday evening with him. I felt as if I had received the Grand Cross of the Legion of Honour, and of course the next Sunday evening I presented myself at the 'Conservatoire', where Cherubini lived, trembling with emotion. The veneration I felt for him must have been strongly depicted on my face, for he received me smiling and endeavoured, by speaking of the pleasure I had given to his son—which pleasure he hoped soon to enjoy also—to encourage and set me at my ease.[1] No easy task, for only in the presence of Beethoven could I have felt the same emotion. His old friend Berton, the once greatly-renowned composer, was with him ('les inséparables' they were called), and greeted me with equal kindness. Cherubini had a great regard for my former master, Rinck, also for G. Weber. After some conversation, of which they formed the subject, I was requested to play one of Beethoven's sonatas, Cherubini professing to be but little acquainted with them, which I found to be the truth by his asking for certain movements, even for whole sonatas, over again not only on this but on many subsequent occasions, for to my intense satisfaction I was invited to repeat my visit. Most of the sonatas I had then the privilege of playing in the presence of Cherubini and Berton were evidently new to them, somewhat to my astonishment, but there could be no doubt about the interest with which they listened to them—an interest demonstrated solely by their silent attention and the requests for repeats, for not once did Cherubini make a remark on the beauty or the character of the works, or criticise them in any way. His silence reminded me of the story told of his witnessing the first performance of one of Halévy's operas, from the com-

---

[1] Cherubini was seventy-eight in 1838. He died in 1842.

poser's box. He kept silence there, until after the second act Halévy, his pupil, asked, 'Maestro, have you nothing to say to me?' when Cherubini snarled back, 'I have been listening to you for two hours and *you* have said nothing to *me.*' But in listening to Beethoven's sonatas his silence could certainly not be attributed to a similar cause; that I saw clearly, even by the play of his handsome features, and why should he have asked me to repeat my visits, had it not been for the interest he felt in these sonatas, which seemed to grow the more I played of them?

Sayings of his, like the above to Halévy, were currently quoted at the time and made him the terror of most people who had to deal with him. There seemed to be no actual 'méchanceté' in him, only an inability to calculate the effect of his words, as in the case of the young man who applied for admission into the operatic class of the Conservatoire, but was so ill-favoured by nature that the professors thought it would be a kindness to him to deter him from trying his luck on the stage. But who was to tell him in a delicate way? Cherubini volunteered to do so, sent for the young man, and said, 'Dear sir, the Conservatoire regrets to be unable to accept you as a pupil because—you are too ugly.' That was his manner of softening a rude blow.

My evenings at the Conservatoire were greatly enjoyed by me, and if Cherubini was reticent in expressing an opinion on Beethoven, he could talk enthusiastically about Gluck, Spontini, and music as an art and a science. About Rossini and the whole school of his followers, then in the ascendant, he could become very sarcastic; it was a topic carefully to be avoided. And so was the mention of the name of Berlioz, who had already become one of my friends. But of him later.

Letters

Translated from the German

Paris: October, 1836

My dearest Parents—At last I have arrived in good health and safety in this huge Paris! am already established in a lodging, have hired a piano, and in short am quite settled. All I shall tell you of my journey is, that I rested a day and a night at Metz, and just as long at Chalons, that I am none the worse, but rather fatigued and stiff, as one cannot help being after such a journey. This must be my whole description of it, as I have more important things to tell you, and especially to you, dear father—viz. about money matters. I shall explain everything fully, and then beg you to enter into it as fully in your answer.

The night before I left Darmstadt, Rinck received an answer from Schlesinger, of Paris, which was very unsatisfactory on the whole; he said nothing at all about Kalkbrenner, and as to Chopin and Liszt, that they took pupils,but were both very much occupied. At the end of the letter he said: 'Living here is rather costly, but if a young man is economical he can live well for 200 frs. a month.' You can easily understand that this gave me a great shock, but as I heard at the same time that Schlesinger lived in great style in Paris (which is a fact), and perhaps judged of others by himself, I took comfort. Now that I am here, I see that it is not the living that is so dear, but, what with lessons, hire of piano, &c., that it will not be possible for me to manage on less than 200 frs. a month. This will give you as little pleasure as it gives me; but above all, do not think that I would treat it lightly—far from it. All my good-humour has gone to the deuce. I will explain more clearly how it is that I need so much. You know that, unfortunately, I am not very robust, and therefore require good and wholesome food. Now I hear from all sides that it would be very cheap to dine at restaurants, but that I must not be surprised if I am sometimes ill in consequence, as they do not cook fresh food every day, but often warm up what is left, even when it is half-spoilt. To get food and lodging in a private house is impossible here, as I am told, so I have taken a room in this hotel, the landlady being a German, and dine at the table d'hôte, which is very good without being brilliant—rather like home cooking, my board and lodging coming to 100 frs. a month. This, according to Tilemann and Rumpe, is very cheap for Paris (in Prussian money it is 26 thalers 26 gr.). Now, I have no wood for the winter, which seems to be frightfully dear, and here neither coal nor turf is used. Then there is the washing. What these last two may cost I do not yet know. Piano hire is exceedingly expensive. As I am here for the purpose of studying the piano, I had to get, if not a good one, at least not a very bad one. I have found a tolerable instrument for 20 frs. a month; I could get none cheaper, even the worst were 15 frs. a month. Here we have come to 120 frs. Now for the lessons. How much they will cost I do not yet know. Kalkbrenner comes back at the end of this week, and I shall go to him at once. It is still doubtful, however, whether he will give me lessons. It seems he is enormously rich, and troubles himself very little with teaching; but I still have hope. Chopin and Liszt charge 20 frs. a lesson; Kalkbrenner, as I have heard, only 10 to 12 frs.; but I do not know if he makes an exception in favour of those who are studying professionally. Should he take 10 frs., if I go to him twice a week, as you desired, it will make 80 frs. a month, which, added to the 120, comes to a total of 200 frs. That leaves me not a penny of pocket money to go to the theatre and hear the great operas. This calculation certainly tends to destroy one's courage. There remains one hope for me—that of giving lessons. Here in Paris, the most second-rate lessons are paid 5 frs. an hour, and good teachers easily get from 8 to 12 frs. a lesson. Should I succeed in finding a few pupils, I could manage very well without greater sacrifices. Mainzer told me that four weeks ago he had been asked for a teacher for two pupils, who would have paid 12 frs. Had I been here I could have got them. At the same time he told me they were rare, as the competition was so very keen. As soon as he hears of any more he will let me know. Perhaps I shall succeed when I am a little better known here, for which I think I shall not have long to wait, as an uncle of Tilemann's and a Dr. Düringe (a German), to whom I had letters from Darmstadt, have promised to introduce me to several families. Most of all Kalkbrenner could help me to get known. Supposing I should succeed, in a month or two, to give one lesson a day even at 6 frs., it would make 150 frs. a month;

that would already be a great help. We may draw the following conclusions from these calculations: if, with the help of God and Kalkbrenner's aid, I should succeed in becoming a good pianist, I cannot fail, in this huge and wealthy Paris, to get more pupils and at a higher price. If, later on, I should get four pupils a day at 10 frs. each (which is very little in comparison with the first-rate pianists, and even with Mainzer, who can be nothing very extraordinary, as he has no name whatever in other countries, and who all charge 20 frs.), we get a monthly income of 1,040 frs.; if I spend 250 frs. there remains a clear balance of nearly 800 frs., or about 9,600 frs. a year. This result is grand, but not at all impossible. You can calculate what a man like Chopin must earn who gives eight or nine lessons a day at 20 frs. In three months' time I shall surely find out if my calculations are correct or not. Should they be so, then, dear father, I have the project, which you will certainly approve, of making Paris my headquarters for a length of time; for tell me any town in Germany, or anywhere else, where it would be possible to earn so much, and at the same time have such opportunities of perfecting oneself in musical, and almost all other respects, as in Paris. Of course, let us not forget that all this depends upon an *if,* but an *if* that may very easily come true. Now I shall leave this chapter, only begging you very earnestly to write to me fully on the subject.

As I have still room, I will chat a little with you, my unspeakably beloved ones, but of what? If I speak of myself, I can only tell you that I have the intensest longing for you and for my own country. Oh, how beautiful, how celestially beautiful, to be at home and in the midst of one's loved ones! What is Paris, with all its luxury and brilliancy, with its crowds of people in the dark and narrow streets where sun and fresh air hardly ever penetrate, with its slow-flowing, turbid Seine, compared with our lovely little valley with its pleasant little town, its clear and merrily-flowing river, its fresh air and brilliant sunshine, with its flowering meadows and green hedges and bushes, where nightingales and finches still sing their joyous song, long since driven away from here by the bustling multitudes whose only thought is gain! Each time I recall all this to mind I cannot keep back the tears. Could I but once walk hand-in-hand with you, the little ones and the dogs playing before us; through the garden, then

by the fields to Alten Hagen; then back by the way of lovely
Wiedey—only once!

. . . Farewell: write soon and at great length. Greet all relations and friends, embrace the two children, think very often of
your loving Carl

Paris: October 18, 1836

Dearest Parents—

. . . I practise nearly the whole day long, and hardly
anything but exercises, shakes, scales, and so on, and the rest of
the time, for it is impossible to play without ceasing, I go over,
and put into order, the work I did with Rinck, or, if ever *it stops
raining for a moment*, I take a run through Paris and visit its sights.
So far I have taken no lessons, but hope to do so in a few days, but
not from Kalkbrenner. I shall tell you the whole story. The day
after Kalkbrenner's return I went to see him at eleven o'clock; he
happened to be at home, and I was shown into an ante-room,
where there were several people already assembled; when he
had kept us waiting a considerable time, he appeared, wrapped
in an ample dressing-gown. After he had spoken for a short time
to the persons standing nearest to him, he came towards me; I
stepped forward and was beginning to explain my business, but
as soon as he heard I intended to become a musician, and had
studied composition with Rinck, he asked me to wait until he
had dismissed the rest of the company. I was pleased at this, as it
would enable me to speak to him undisturbed. It lasted a good
long time, but finally he had despatched them all, and I was able
to make my request. When I had done speaking, he said he
regretted very much that it was at present impossible for him to
comply with my wish; he had been seriously ill, had only just
returned from the Baths, and was still so weak that his doctor
had strictly forbidden him to talk much, a thing quite
unavoidable in giving lessons—in fact, he did look very ill. He
had his class at the Conservatoire, which he could not give up,
and that tired him so, that he had been obliged to give up all
other lessons. It was now my turn to express regret. Then he said
he would like to hear me play, to see how far I had got on, and
that he could perhaps recommend a teacher to me. He took me
into his sitting-room, where there was a most beautiful grand
piano, and I played him his own 'Effusio Musica'. He made

several remarks about the *tempo*, and said several times, 'very good', 'first rate', until I got to a part where both hands had scales in octaves during several pages; when I had finished them he stopped me, and asked why I played the octaves with my arms and not from my wrists? 'You are quite out of breath,' he said (which was the case); *he* could play scales in octaves for an hour without the least fatigue; and why had God given us wrists? He was sure, if the Almighty had ever played the piano, He would play from the wrist! He made several other remarks; he said I held my fingers rather too high, I must hold them closer to the keys, especially in *legato* passages, to make them more finished, and obtain altogether a rounder and more ringing tone; and as to the expression, he gave me a good deal of advice, all very good, and worthy to be followed. He then played part of the piece I had played, to make it clear to me; after this, he began another, and altogether *played for me more than half-an-hour*. You can imagine my delight; it was the first time I had ever heard a celebrated musician, and this half-hour has been of the greatest use to me. In Kalkbrenner's playing there reigns a clearness, a distinctness, and neatness that are astonishing; in octave scales he has an immense facility and precision, especially in the left hand; then he has a special mode of handling the piano, particularly in melodious passages, which makes a great impression, but which I cannot describe to you; the reason of it lies merely in that he keeps his fingers so closely over the keys. When he had finished, he told me to be very industrious, to avoid the mistakes he had pointed out, and that I would become a first-rate pianist; at present I should go to Osborne,[1] his best pupil, and who had quite his method of teaching (Mr. Elbers and I have played something of Osborne's, and, as far as I recollect, we liked it very much); I should tell him that Kalkbrenner has sent me to him and begged him to give me lessons; when I had worked with him for some time then *he, Kalkbrenner, would give me some lessons with the greatest pleasure.* As often as I had studied a piece with Osborne I should come and play it to him, and if there was still anything wanting, he would point it out to me. I must also come and see him from time to time. That was kind, was it not? and I shall certainly not fail to take him at his word.

[1] George Alexander Osborne, Irish pianist and composer.

Next day I went to Osborne (Tuesday, this day week); he also was out of town, and only returned on Saturday. On Sundays in Paris no one is ever to be found at home, so I went on Monday, yesterday, and luckily found him at home. He received me very amiably, and when I had told him my tale, he said I put him in a great perplexity; that he gave lessons from early morning till night, and still he was most unwilling to refuse me. After a little more conversation he asked me to play something; I did so, and he praised and blamed exactly in the same way as Kalkbrenner had done; then he asked my address, and said he would write to me in a few days to say whether he had found it possible to arrange to give me lessons, and in this letter he would give me all particulars; should there be any evening parties with music, he would introduce me with pleasure. I am therefore awaiting this letter; should he delay too long, which I do not expect, I shall go to some one else. I have been here more than a fortnight, and have only been able to study by myself; but soon after my arrival, Mr. Probst of Leipzig, who lives here, and whose acquaintance I made through Mr. Tilemann's uncle, told me that if I had not learnt patience before, I should learn it here, and, in truth, it seems so. Neither Meyerbeer nor Hiller are in Paris, so I cannot deliver my letters to them. As to hearing many good works, it is not as we expected; at all the theatres there are only small operettas and ballets, even at the Grand Opera, where all the best and newest operas are generally given. A new ballet, 'La Fille du Danube', will probably have a hundred successive performances, so much does it please the Parisians; so there is but a poor prospect of hearing good music. All these things are not calculated to banish my bad humour; on the contrary, my longing for you and for my beautiful, peaceful birthplace grows even stronger. *Christmas and New Year! O Gott!*

The only thing I am looking forward to is that Mainzer has promised to procure me the opportunity of often hearing Chopin and Liszt. I hope he will keep his word, for it would be of the greatest use to me.

Carl

Paris: November, 1836

Dearest Parents—. . . I must tell you that, God be praised and thanked, I have begun with Osborne, and have already had three lessons—one per week, which *is amply sufficient* (ten francs each). . . My manner of playing has to be entirely altered—not so much the expression, as my right reverend Aunt Christina, with an air of wisdom, opined; on the contrary, he paid me great compliments on this point. But it seems I had an abominable tone. You will, perhaps, not quite understand this, but as soon as I get back to Hagen I shall make it clear to you. I am making great progress already on this point, and during my last lesson he said several times: 'Je suis fort content de vous, vous êtes très-bon musicien.'

I doubt whether, London excepted, there is another town in the world that can compare with Paris in any respect. Louis Flashoff would say it is a 'Gegenstand'—his favourite expression for anything grand. It gives me a curious sensation as often as I look from any height upon this immense agglomeration of stone. As far as the eye can reach, nothing but the sky and houses. One can never see the whole of Paris— some part is always lost in the distance. Everything in Paris is on a grand scale—manners and customs as well as the town itself; N.B., the prices too. Such a quantity of palaces, monuments, arches of triumph, one finds nowhere else. To describe it all is impossible; I should require much more time and much more paper. The finest building in Paris, and perhaps in all Europe, is the new church of the Madeleine. Only it hardly does for a church, nor was it originally meant for one. Napoleon, who began it, intended it for a Temple of Fame. It is built in the same Greek style (I believe after a temple of Minerva or Apollo at Athens), and so makes a curious impression in the midst of the modern houses and palaces that surround it. In Paris one has the best opportunities of studying the differences between the old Gothic and the Grecian styles, the first represented by the venerable cathedral of Notre Dame, and the second by this Temple of the Madeleine. Both are sublime masterworks, but what an endless difference! The thrill one feels on entering a Gothic church like Cologne Cathedral is not experienced at the sight of this great temple, but a feeling of admiration for the grand old Greeks and for the days of antiquity passes through one. Under the high arches and vaulted roof of a Gothic cathedral one feels a certain sense (I at least do) of oppression, and breathes more freely when one returns to the open air. In this Greek temple everything is calculated to produce an agreeable and cheerful sensation; the whole building seems so light, even smart, if that expression is not too trivial. In short, it represents the ideal of spirited beauty. So one could never picture a Gothic cathedral in a fine open landscape, but one can think of such a temple in the midst of the old Grecian land, with laurel groves and myrtle woods. Then it makes an unpleasant sensation to see the modish young bucks in their frock coats, white cuffs, kid gloves and walking sticks, wandering among the Corinthian columns and up the grand flight of steps. At every moment one expects to see a tall, stately Grecian figure step out and drive away these dandies, as Christ drove the money-lenders out of the temple . . .

Paris: November 28, 1836

Dearest Parents—

. . . Now I shall tell you how it befell with the Leipzig letters, and, thank God, have only good tidings to give. All those to whom I was recommended received me with so much heartiness, not, as so often happens, with mere empty politeness, that I soon saw the great value of an introduction from Uncle Harkort. Especially Mr. Kalle and Mr. Thurneyssen were extraordinarily amiable; the first has invited me at least five or six times to dinner, and every Sunday evening to tea, and both he and his charming and beautiful young wife are always so kind and friendly, that I am in high spirits the whole day previous to going there. I always meet a large company there, consisting of French, Germans, English and Americans, and spend many a pleasant hour. Kalle has also told me, if ever I am in any difficulty, to apply to him at once and he would advise and help efficaciously. I have dined twice at the Thurneyssen's and am invited to a soirée for every Friday evening. I enjoy myself *very much* at their house also, and have made several pleasant acquaintances there, amongst them that of M. Scherbius, who is going to introduce me the day after to-morrow to Ferdinand Ries, who happens to be in Paris, at which I am immensely delighted; should he ask me to play I shall choose his own dear 'Am Rhein, Am Rhein'. The Thurneyssens must be very rich people; although the Kalles display great elegance, it is nothing to be compared to the luxury of the others; it is quite indescribable, but when I come home I shall have wonderful things to tell you of it, as well as of the tone and mode of Paris, that one has always read so much about.

Baron Eichthal also received me very well, and of him I have the greatest hopes from a musical point of view; he invited me a week ago, in a very amiable note, to dine with him on Wednesday (the day after to-morrow) and said he hoped to introduce me then to his friend *Chopin!* So far I have neither seen nor heard Chopin, as all the soirées and concerts at which such artists play are only beginning now or a little later on. I have little fear but that once presented to Chopin by Eichthal he will invite me to his own house, and then I shall hear him not only once but several times. I also hope to be introduced to Liszt shortly, and Mr. Tilemann's uncle is going to make me known to Herz. So, by degrees, I shall get to know these people; things do not go quickly in Paris; one requires a boundless patience; so too with regard to the giving of lessons, which I thought would be so easy before I came. Up to the present there seems no prospect; principally as I do not know enough French to be able to teach. I hear from all sides that it is very easy to make a large fortune in Paris, when one has bitten one's way through, has made oneself known, and acquired a certain fame in the town; then every one rushes to you, and your hours are measured in gold; but it takes a pretty long time before one gets so far.

All the same, I still think it would be best, after I have quite completed my education, to return here for a considerable length of time; where so many others have been so fortunate, I, too, may perhaps succeed. I have now heard Kalkbrenner several times, and have paid him another visit, and shall go again one of these days, as I have studied twelve grand Etudes of his with Osborne, which I want to play to him. Last Sunday I heard him at a concert at the Hôtel de Ville; he played twice, first the Rondo, 'Gage d'Amitié' (which Mrs. Hennecke made me a present of), and then variations on a theme of Bellini's. I was very glad to hear him play a piece I knew, and to be able to discover in how much I am still wanting. He began the allegro of the Rondo at a speed that made my hair stand on end; he carried it on at the same pace, which he even increased towards the close, with such a bell-like clearness, and such great expression,

71

that I cannot understand how any one could do it better; and still, Chopin and Liszt stand higher than Kalkbrenner. When next I see him I shall remind him of his promise to give me lessons, but should he not be willing to do so yet, I shall not insist, as Osborne's teaching pleases me very much, and Kalkbrenner's lessons will be more useful to me later on, when I have studied more; on no account shall I leave Paris without taking a few lessons from him, so as to be able to call myself his pupil.

You write to me, dear father, that by the end of January I shall most likely, or certainly, have to return home; I know that my stay here costs a terrible amount of money, and that it cannot go on long, so I shall say no word against it, and I shall rejoice to be with you again; but at the same time I am convinced that the object of my coming here will only have been half accomplished if I go away so soon; I should only have had altogether thirteen or fourteen lessons, and have arrived at the point where lessons from Kalkbrenner would be of the greatest use. I am making great progress, and Osborne praises me very much; he told me that during the winter I should study a concerto with him, and I believe that if I could thoroughly and perfectly study a concerto with such a master, so as to be able to play it anywhere, I should hardly need further lessons, but could perfect myself on the model of the great artists whom I have the opportunity of hearing; but, I believe, *only then*. However, if I must return home so soon I shall say no word against it, but shall even rejoice.

November 29

I had got so far yesterday when the dinner-bell called me (at half past five). This morning at nine o'clock, dressed in my best, I went to Meyerbeer; at the door I met a Berliner, Rudolfi (whom I only know by name), who had also come to pay his respects. In the anteroom the servant received us with a shrug of his shoulders, and said he did not think we could be admitted, as Meyerbeer[1] was composing, and had sent away a lot of people already; he went away and shortly came back with a very polite

[1] Jakob Meyerbeer (1791-1864) had been court musician to the Grand Duke of Darmstadt early in his career. His opera *Robert le Diable*, first performed in Paris in 1831, had won him world-wide renown, and *Les Huguenots* had been given its first performance earlier in 1836.

message that his master was so very busy that he could not possibly be disturbed, but begged us not to take it amiss, and to come without fail to-morrow morning at nine o'clock. This I shall certainly not fail to do, as I am convinced that I shall be well received, as was my friend Mangold, who also brought him a letter from Rinck, and whose compositions he examined and corrected, and to whom he also often sends tickets for his operas. Most likely you do not know that Mangold is in Paris. I luckily persuaded him to come, but as he could not leave Darmstadt with me, he followed a fortnight later; we see each other very seldom, as he lives at half-an-hour's distance from me. This is one of the disadvantages of Paris, the difficulty of seeing even one's best friends on account of the great distances; it would have been impossible for us to live together, the one playing the piano and the other the violin; we should have disturbed each other and made a veritable cat's concert of it.

You, dear mother, wish to be assured that I am not freezing here; I can do so. Firstly, in my room I have no open fire, but a stove, a remarkable one made of *porcelaine,* but which warms the room very well; there is a fireplace, but as the landlord offered me a stove I accepted without hesitation; an open fire looks very nice and cosy, but one gets roasted on one side and frozen on the other. Second, although the weather is very unpleasant, always raining and windy, it has been so warm that, although we are close upon December 1, I need no fire, but at the beginning of the month it was so cold that I could not do without one; I only wish it would remain warm, for wood costs a terrible deal of money here, and coal is unknown; two logs of wood cost almost a franc. . .

Carl

Paris: December 2, 1836

Beloved Parents—

. . . The morning after having written to you I went again to Meyerbeer, and was at once admitted. As I expected, Meyerbeer was extremely kind and amiable. He kept me more than half an hour, inquired after Rinck and as to all my studies, asked if I had yet composed anything, how I got on in Paris, if I had heard the most eminent pianists, of whom Liszt was the very first, and so on. When I told him that I had neither seen nor heard Liszt, he said I must call again in a few days, in the morning, and he would give me an introduction to him; Liszt was a very nice young man, who would certainly receive me very kindly. How pleased I am that Meyerbeer should give me an introduction to that original fellow Liszt I cannot describe. This also is all very good and satisfactory.

The same evening I went to dine with Baron Eichthal, where I was very cordially treated, and where I heard—*Chopin.* That was beyond all words. The few senses I had have quite left me. I could have jumped into the Seine. Everything I hear now seems so insignificant, that I would rather not hear it at all. Chopin! He is no man, he is an angel, a god (or what can I say more?). Chopin's compositions played by Chopin! That is a joy never to be surpassed. I shall describe his playing another time. Kalkbrenner compared to Chopin is a child. I say this with the completest conviction. During Chopin's playing I could think of nothing but elves and fairy dances, such a wonderful impression do his compositions make. There is nothing to remind one that it is a human being who produces this music. It seems to descend from heaven—so pure, and clear, and spiritual. I feel a thrill each time I think of it. If Liszt plays *still better*, then the devil take me if I don't shoot myself on the spot. Chopin is moreover a charming, delightful creature. He talked to me a long time, gave me his address and the permission to go and see him often, a permission he will not have given in vain. . .

Carolus

Paris: December 19, 1836

Dearest Parents—For the last time this year I sit down to write to you . . . there is, in fact, no need for our writing much to each other, as I expect and hope to be with you in nine or ten weeks, and how soon they will pass! But first let me thank you, dear father, for having granted me another month. I know that it will be difficult for you, and therefore my gratitude is all the greater. I shall do my utmost to make the month of great profit to me. Of what shall I write? As I know that musical matters interest you most, I shall begin with them, and tell you that I have heard Liszt.

Meyerbeer gave me a kind, two-pages-long letter of introduction to him, which did not fail in its effect. When I went for the first time I did not find Liszt at home, and was told he only received on Monday and Friday afternoons from 2 to 5 o'clock. As I have a lesson on Fridays, I had to wait till Monday—a week to-day—when I went towards 3 o'clock. How curious I was to see this man, who has so remarkable a fame, you can easily imagine, especially as he has the reputation, even in his outward appearance, of being a most original creature; and so I found him. Liszt is the most original being in existence. When I entered I found an assembly of thirty or forty persons, among them many of the first artists of Paris, and even several ladies, who had come to pay him homage (I had noticed a great number of carriages at the door). He, the fêted Liszt, came to me at once, and I gave him my letter. When he opened it he glanced at once at the signature, and seeing the name of Meyerbeer he shook me again by the hand and kindly bade me sit down. I did not accept the invitation, as there were forty persons in the room and only ten chairs, all of which were occupied. He did not notice it, spoke to me a little while, and then sprang off to some one else. I then had time to look at him carefully, and saw that I had not been told too much about the originality of his outward appearance. His aspect is truly remarkable. He is tall and very thin, his face very small and pale, his forehead remarkably high and beautiful; he wears his perfectly lank hair so long that it spreads over his shoulders, which looks very odd, for when he gets a bit excited and gesticulates, it falls right over his face and one sees nothing but his nose. He is very negligent in his attire, his coat looks as if it had just been thrown on, he wears no cravat, only a narrow white collar. This curious figure is in perpetual motion: now he stamps with his feet, now waves his arms in the air, now he does this, now that. My hope of hearing him play in his own house was deceived. He has *no instrument!* I remained a few hours with him, until one after another the guests had left, then *(Donnerwetter!* here is a terrible blot! How it came I know not, but to copy the letter would be too tedious, so take blot and all!) I took my leave also. He accompanied me to the ante-room, and said that on Sunday (yesterday) he was giving a concert at the Conservatoire: that he would have given me a ticket with the greatest pleasure had he a single one left to dispose of, but he had given all his free tickets away, but if I cared to go to the rehearsal I must be there on Saturday morning at 9 o'clock, and that I

75

must also come and see him very often.

I have now heard him twice: at the rehearsal, where he only played once, and at the concert three times, for I invested five francs in a ticket. When I heard him first I sat speechless for a quarter of an hour afterwards, in such a stupor of amazement had the man put me. Such execution, such limitless—truly limitless—execution no one else can possess. He plays sometimes so as to make your hair stand on end! He who has not heard Liszt can have no conception—literally no conception —of what his playing is. After having heard him my resolution was taken. 'Now you go straight home,' I said to myself, 'and grind frightfully for a couple of years, and if at the end of the time you have accomplished anything fit, you may come back here.' And so it shall be.

When I have worked very hard at home I shall certainly then return to Paris, I like it so well; so well, that already I could wish to stay here for ever; and Paris is also the place where one can earn money. . .

Carolus

3

Paris, 1838–48

In the winter of 1838–9 Stephen Heller[1] arrived in Paris, which makes an epoch in my life. A friendship sprang up between us almost at once, which endured uninterruptedly to the end of his days in 1888, and had a most decided influence upon my intellectual development. Only those who have known him as intimately as I have (and I doubt if there are any) can appreciate the high quality of his gifts, the superiority of his intelligence, and the soundness of his judgment in all matters musical, artistic, and literary. He brought few of his compositions with him, and, in fact, nearly all his works date from Paris, but these few revealed the real musician, the original thinker, and had already attracted Schumann's attention, with whom Heller corresponded frequently. I was happy to meet a man whose whole soul was wrapped up in music—as my own was—and the long hours we spent together at the piano playing duets form some of my most cherished recollections. It was during these *séances* in my humble lodgings in the Rue Notre Dame de Lorette that we made acquaintance with and revelled in the beauties of Schubert's great C major symphony, then recently discovered and published as a pianoforte duet.[2] It was a revelation to us, and we were never tired of playing it through. But the same

[1] The pianist Stephen Heller (1814–88) had a high reputation as a teacher and composer. His compositions had an influence on later French composers, among them Fauré, but are today rarely heard.

[2] Mendelssohn conducted the first performance at Leipzig in March 1839.

77

was the case with all the great compositions for orchestra, or orchestra with chorus, arranged in a similar form. How often we must have played Beethoven's symphonies it is impossible to tell, and how we enjoyed them! All the more as the opportunities of hearing them performed by the orchestra were then most rare, the Concerts du Conservatoire[1] only bringing forward two or three during a season, so that certain of them, for instance, Nos. 4, 7, and 9, were heard perhaps once in three or four years. In 1839 neither Heller nor I had ever heard the Choral Symphony performed, and were therefore all the more eager to study it closely. Such a performance was approached with a certain solemnity. When our means—slender at that time—permitted, a bottle of champagne was sent for and drunk during the performance as on a festive occasion. But here, for once, we felt the inadequacy of the piano; much as we admired the three first movements, we could not understand the finale, hard as we tried; it left on us a disagreeable impression, somewhat akin to sea-sickness, in spite of which we renewed again and again our endeavour to fathom it, but with no better result.

Heller was a remarkable pianist, but shrank from playing in public, and perhaps he had not the gift to impress a large audience. There was a singular modesty and reticence in his playing of his own works, an indication only of expression and *nuance*, as if he felt shy of telling all the secrets of his heart. This shyness, however, left him entirely when he was improvising, a gift in which he excelled all great musicians that I have known. The change that came over him and his execution in such moments, or hours, was marvellous. As a rule he was not a very great master of technique, but when improvising all difficulties seemed to vanish, and it is certain that if he had been able to place before him in print what he accomplished in these moments of inspiration he would have stared, and it would

[1] Founded by François Habeneck (1781-1849), a violinist before he became a conductor, in 1828.

have taken him weeks of hard study to play what had seemed so easy. Whether he improvised quite freely, or on subjects self-chosen or given to him, he was equally fascinating, dominating his listeners and pouring out a wealth of ideas of which his published compositions give no idea. He had an extraordinary faculty of combining the most dissimilar themes, and proved it once—the only time, I believe, he ever improvised in public—where the opening of 'Don Giovanni', 'Notte e giorno faticar', Pedrillo's 'Viva Bacco, Bacco viva', from 'Il Seraglio', and his own 'Wanderstunden', were given to him, and after the one and the other had been treated most ingeniously for some time, they were all three, or the semblance of them, heard at the same time, a feat so difficult of execution that it would have required long practice on the part of any pianist to master it, and here it was accomplished spontaneously. The occasion was a visit he paid to England in 1862, of which I may speak here, as it is connected with his talent for improvisation. I had heard from him that he was what is commonly called 'hard up', and in order to replenish his exhausted exchequer had obtained for him several engagements in England and induced him to give a concert in Manchester. Everywhere we played duets for two pianos, Heller being too nervous to appear alone; but for the Manchester concert, which I was most anxious should have a good result, I had insisted on his including in the programme an 'Improvisation on subjects given by the audience.' After a hard fight he had submitted, and my expectations of a crowded house were fully realised. I little knew that a catastrophe was impending, from which fortunately I was able to save Heller. On the day previous to the concert a charming young lady, who with her sister took lessons from me, asked me, 'Is it really true that Heller is going to improvise?' 'Yes, it is part of the programme,' was my answer. 'Oh, how droll! and may any one give a subject?' 'Certainly, anybody that can think of one.' 'So, if I said—sponge, would that do?' I cannot imagine what the consequence would have been, but the improvisation would have been 'sponged' out.

I return to my narrative of very happy times, made principally so by my friendship with Heller and by the interest with which I and a few other intimate musical friends watched and enjoyed his productions. By the time Heller came to Paris I had already made a good many friends and could be of some use to him by introducing him to people he wished to know. In my turn I owe him some most interesting acquaintances. My circumstances were gradually improving, thanks to the number of my pupils increasing constantly, so that I was able to move into better quarters, in the Rue d'Amsterdam, where I first began to have a few musical evenings at home, reunions of friends, such as Berlioz, Heller, Ernst, Batta (the accomplished and refined violoncellist), Artôt, known as 'le bel Artôt', Delsarte, the marvellous tenor without a voice, and several others.[1] On one evening Artôt proposed that we should play the Kreutzer Sonata, and we did so. Now Artôt, most elegant violinist and most successful performer though he was, was entirely out of his element in such music, which was so painfully evident that when he had left us rather early, Ernst sprang up and said, 'Come, Hallé, let us play the *Kreutzer*!' He played it magnificently, and I have never better understood than on that evening how much depends upon the power of interpretation; how the want of it can deprive the finest work of its charm and interest.

From the Rue d'Amsterdam I moved to the Rue Laffitte, where I had charming, quiet rooms with a view upon some beautiful gardens, and here it was that Heller first brought Heinrich Heine to me. They knew each other from being both contributors to the 'Augsburger Allgemeine Zeitung', Germany's most important paper

---

[1] Heinrich Wilhelm Ernst (1814-64) was a Moravian violinist who lived in Paris from 1832 to 1838. Alexandre Artôt (1815-45) was the Belgian violinist for whom Berlioz wrote his *Rêverie et Caprice* op. 8 (1839). For more about Delsarte see page 96.

then. Heine, then only about forty-two years of age, of handsome and winning appearance, strong and healthy, with no indication of the sufferings that were to be his fate later on, was, of course, a most welcome guest. He came often, always with Heller—in fact, I cannot remember a single occasion on which our trio developed into a quartet, and many were our discussions on music, in which he took great interest—perhaps without really understanding, as some of his remarks seemed to show. I had brought with me, after an excursion to Germany, the book of songs by Mendelssohn, in which the first is the setting of Heine's 'Auf Flügeln des Gesanges'. I spoke of it with enthusiasm to Heine, who came the same evening with Heller to the Rue Laffitte, most eager to hear this version of his poem. I had a feeble, but not altogether disagreeable tenor voice, and sang the 'Lied' to him with all the expression I was capable of, and certainly correctly as regards the music. Great was my astonishment, and Heller's also, when at the conclusion he said in a disappointed tone, 'There is no melody in it.' As there is nothing but melody in it, we long puzzled over the riddle—What sort of melody may satisfy a poet when he hears his own words sung? An insoluble one, I am afraid.

Irresistibly charming was Heine when, the conversation flagging, which often happens when three smokers sit together, he would, after a more or less long silence, suddenly recite one of his shorter poems, clothing it with undreamt-of beauty by his manner of delivery. We sat in mute wonder, and it seemed quite natural that he should add musingly in a half unconscious tone: 'Beautiful!' The oddity of the remark, coming from himself, never once struck us: it was so perfectly true. Our relations remained for years the most friendly; then suddenly and unexpectedly he showed the cloven hoof. I had already begun to give concerts and had been treated most kindly by him, when one day, after one of them which he had attended, I met him on the Boulevard, went up to him to shake hands, and was cut dead. There was no mistake, and often as we met after that he took no notice of me. At that time he wrote to the 'Augsburger Zeitung' that I was a small prophet whom the whale would have spat out promptly if it had swallowed him. I had reason to believe that a mistake made in the tickets sent him for my concert was the source of his anger, and was extremely sorry for it; but as he ought to have known that the mistake could not have originated with me, I was too proud to seek an explanation. So we passed each other for many months without so much as a look, until one day, meeting on the same Boulevard, he came up to me, shook my hand warmly in the old friendly manner, and after a few commonplace questions, asked: 'Were you at Doehler's concert yesterday?' and hearing that I had not been there, he added *à brûle-pourpoint,* 'I do not like him. No, no; to hear somebody who plays *really* well, one must come to you!' 'Hallo!' I said, 'and what about the whale?' Upon which he laughed most heartily, shook my hand again, and departed without further explanation. After that we were the same old friends again.

Towards the end of the year 1839 Heller brought one evening to my rooms a young musician, my senior only by six years, whose acquaintance he had made through Maurice Schlesinger, and who, as he told me in a side whisper, stood in great need of kindness and assistance. The name of this young musician was Richard Wagner, a name which at that time meant nothing to us, as we were in absolute ignorance of the talents he might or might not be endowed with. We knew that he was in great straits, had unsuccessfully applied for an appointment as chorus singer in a small theatre, and for his living made all kinds of arrangements for Schlesinger, even to an arrangement of Halévy's 'La Reine de Chypre' for *two flutes,* to which Heller suggested the addition of a big drum. Wagner himself used to laugh at this occupation, the result of dire necessity; and we, never having seen or heard a note of his own compositions, took it almost for granted that he was not fit for much more. He was no pianist or he might have given us some idea of his own work. He rarely spoke of his aspirations, but when he did so, it was usually in a strain which made us wonder if, as the phrase goes, he was 'all there.' We liked him as a most frank, amiable, and lively companion, modest and full of enthusiasm for all that is beautiful in art. And he felt evidently at home with us. He came often to the Rue Laffitte. Heller improvised, I played or we played duets, and I remember that one evening when I had played to them Schumann's 'Carnaval',[1] then quite new, we three indited a letter of thanks to the composer, which letter I saw more than forty years later in the hands of his widow. In 1876, when I met him at Bayreuth, his first words alluded to the pleasant evenings with Heller at my rooms in Paris. What an immense change had taken place! What a difference there was between the man of 1839 and the man of 1876!

Schlesinger, the proprietor of the 'Gazette Musicale', the most important musical paper in France, gave to the subscribers annually a few concerts with a view to increasing their number, and in the spring of 1840 he included in the programme an overture by his then *protégé*, Richard Wagner[2]. The overture was called 'Christoph Colomb', and as it was the first time we were to hear a specimen of our friend's works, we were naturally very curious, and attended the concert with great expectations. The result was disastrous. Whether it was that the performance, for want of rehearsals, was most imperfect, or that the style was what we might now call *ultra-Wagnerian*, or for both these reasons joined together, the whole overture struck us as the work of a madman, and we had no opportunity to reconsider our judgment, as 'Christoph Colomb' has never again seen the light. It was not many months after this *fiasco* that we heard with amazement of the great success his opera,

---

[1] *Carnaval* was composed in 1834.
[1] The performance was actually on February 4, 1841. Wagner put the blame for its failure on the incompetent orchestral trumpeters.

'Rienzi', had achieved in Dresden, and still greater was our astonishment when the perusal of the score showed us that the success was perfectly justified. Here was a case of unrecognised merit, if ever there was one—or rather a proof of the difficulties that confront the musician who is a composer. A painter shows his picture and the world judges it. But the composer of an opera may carry the score round with him for years and nobody will be the wiser for it. In after years I met Wagner seldom, and each time found it more difficult to recognise in him the genial, modest young companion I had known so well. His manner of speech had become bombastic, often not to be 'understanded of the people'. In 1862 we met by accident in the ruins of the old castle of Heidelberg. In the previous winter I had given concert performances of Gluck's 'Iphigenia in Tauris', in Manchester, London and other towns with remarkable success. This apparently had interested Wagner greatly, and rather surprised him. He spoke of it at length, and concluded by saying: 'The English are an extraordinary people—*und dennoch weiss ich nicht ob es je bei ihnen zu dem Seufzer kommt, ohne den der Blumenduft der Kunst nicht in den Aether steigt.*' I have quoted this wonderful sentence in the original German, but it may be roughly translated: 'Still, I do not know if ever they arrive at the sigh, without which the aroma of the art does not ascend into space.' Dr. E. Becker, for so many years librarian to H.M. Queen Victoria, was with me on that occasion, and immediately wrote down the sentence in his pocket-book. He never understood it, but felt it was worth preserving.

At Bayreuth, in 1876, during one of the welcome entr'actes, we met in the open air, he being surrounded by a crowd of admirers. It was then that he alluded to the pleasant evenings in Paris, expressed how gratified he was that I, too, had come all the way from England to hear his works, and ended by saying emphatically, 'You see, my dear Hallé, I shall make Bayreuth the centre of civilisation.' 'A noble aim, my dear master,' was my answer. We never met again.

To return to 1838, a year so rich to me in reminiscences. I must say a few words about a man, in his way the most remarkable of his time, Paganini.[1] He was one of the wonders of the world to me, so much had I read and heard about him, and I deeply deplored that he had given up public playing, and—so I was told—even chose his lodgings so that the sound of his violin could not be heard outside. The striking, awe-inspiring, ghost-like figure of Paganini was to be seen nearly every afternoon in the music shop of Bernard Latte, Passage de l'Opéra, where he sat for an hour, enveloped in a long cloak, taking notice of nobody, and hardly ever raising his piercing black eyes. He was one of the sights of Paris, and I had often gone to stare at him with wonder until a friend introduced me to him, and he invited me to visit him, an invitation I accepted most eagerly. I went often, but it would be difficult to relate a single conversation we had together. He sat there, taciturn, rigid, hardly ever moving a muscle of his face, and I sat spellbound, a shudder running through me whenever his uncanny eyes fell upon me. He made me play to him often, mostly by pointing with his bony hand to the piano without speaking, and I could only guess from his repeating the ceremony that he did not dislike it, for never a word of encouragement fell from his lips. How I longed to hear him play it is impossible to describe, perhaps even to imagine. From my earliest childhood I had heard of Paganini and his art as of something supernatural, and there I actually sat opposite to the man himself, but only looking at the hands that had created such wonders. On one never-to-be-forgotten occasion, after I had played and we had enjoyed a long silence, Paganini rose and approached his violin-case. What then passed in me can hardly be imagined; I was all in a tremble, and my heart

---

[1] At this date Paganini was fifty-four. He died two years afterwards.

thumped as if it would burst my chest; in fact, no young swain going to the first rendezvous with his beloved could possibly feel more violent emotions. Paganini opened the case, took the violin out, and began to tune it carefully with his fingers without using the bow; my agitation became almost intolerable. When he was satisfied, and I said to myself, with a lump in my throat, 'Now, now, he'll take the bow!' he carefully put the violin back and shut the case. And that is how I heard Paganini.

The most important friendship I formed at that time (or it may have been at the end of 1837) was that with Hector Berlioz—'le vaillant Hector,' as he was often called—whose powerful dominating personality I was glad to recognise. How I made his acquaintance is now a mystery to me—it seems as if I had always known him—I also wonder often how it was he showed such interest in an artist of so little importance as I then was; he was so kind to me, and, in fact, became my friend. Perhaps it was because we could both speak with the same enthusiasm of Beethoven, Gluck, Weber, even Spontini, and, perhaps, not less because he felt that I had a genuine admiration for his own works. There never lived a musician who adored his art more than did Berlioz; he was, indeed, 'enthusiasm personified.' To hear him speak of, or rave about, a real *chef d'oeuvre*, such as 'Armida', 'Iphigenia', or the C minor Symphony, the pitch of his voice rising higher and higher as he talked, was worth any performance of the same.[1] And what a picture he was at the head of his orchestra, with his eagle face, his bushy hair, his air of command, and glowing with enthusiasm. He was the most perfect conductor that I ever set eyes upon, one who held absolute sway over his troops, and played upon them as a pianist upon the keyboard. But discussion about his genius and his works is superfluous at the present time; even his life is so

---

[1] In an after-dinner speech in Manchester in 1886, Hallé referred to Berlioz's taciturnity. They would sometimes spend an evening together, reading, during which only a few words would be exchanged. At the stroke of ten Berlioz would rise to leave saying: 'This has been a most enjoyable evening, my dear Hallé.'

thoroughly known that I need only relate of him what has come under my personal knowledge.

He also came often to my humble lodgings, and I must say that his visits to me were more frequent than mine to him; for even at that time Madame Berlioz, the once charming and poetic Ophelia, had become somewhat repellent, and it was impossible to imagine her acting or anybody falling in love with her. To her honour it must, however, be said that she upheld Berlioz in his hardest struggles, always ready to endure the greatest privations when it was a question for him to save money enough for the organisation of a concert on a large scale, concerts which seldom left any profit. I had the pleasure of introducing him to Stephen Heller, who soon won his esteem, and remained on friendly terms with him until his death. Berlioz was no executant upon any instrument (for being able to strum a few chords on the guitar does not count), and he was painfully aware how much this was a hindrance to him, and to his knowledge of musical literature, which, indeed, was limited. I was often astonished to find that works, familiar to every pianist, were unknown to him; not merely works written for the piano, such as Beethoven's sonatas, of which he knew but few, but also orchestral works, oratorios, &c., known to the pianist through arrangements, but of which he had not chanced to see a score. Perhaps many undoubted crudities in his works would have been eliminated had he been able to hear them before committing them to paper, for I had several proofs that the eye alone was not sufficient to give him a clear idea of the effect of his musical combinations. Thus at the time when he scored Weber's 'Invitation à la Valse' for the orchestra, he made me play it to him, and when I had come to the point where, after the digression into C major, the theme is resumed in the original key, D flat, he interrupted me with the words, 'Après tout, cela va,' confessing that from the perusal of the piece he had thought the modulation too harsh, and almost impossible. On another occasion, much later, he arrived at my house and eagerly told me he had found a new cadence to end a movement with. 'The last chord,' he said, 'is the chord of G major, and I precede it by the one in B minor.' When I told him there were hundreds of examples of such an ending, he would not believe me, and was greatly astonished when we ·searched for and found them.

In some of the most interesting moments of Berlioz's musical career in Paris I had the privilege of being with him. Thus on December 5, 1837, I went with him to the Hôtel des Invalides to witness the first performance of his 'Requiem', and was, therefore, an eye-witness of what took place on that occasion. Habeneck, after Berlioz the most accomplished *chef d'orchestre* in Paris, conducted by rights, and Berlioz sat in a chair near him. Habeneck, who conducted not only the Grand Opera but also the 'Concerts du Conservatoire', had the habit of now and then putting his conducting stick down and listening complacently to the performance of his orchestra. It was, therefore, perhaps force of habit that made him discard the bâton at the commencement of the 'Tuba mirum', this time not to listen, but leisurely to take a pinch of snuff! To my amazement I suddenly saw Berlioz standing in Habeneck's place and wielding the bâton to the end of the movement. The moment had been a most critical one, four groups of brass instruments, stationed at the four corners of the large orchestra, which with the chorus was placed under the dome in the centre of the building, having to enter successively, and, without Berlioz's determination, disaster must have ensued, thanks to the unfortunate pinch of snuff. Habeneck, after the performance, thanked Berlioz profusely for his timely aid, and admitted that his own thoughtlessness might have caused a break-down, but Berlioz remained persuaded that there had been no thoughtlessness, and that the break-down was intended. I could not believe this, for the simple reason that when such a thing occurs it is always the conductor on whose

Top. Berlioz conducting; satirical
German engraving

Bottom. Liszt playing for charity before the
Emperor Francis Joseph at Budapest, 1872

Chopin; daguerreotype taken shortly
before his death in 1849

Charles Hallé with his first wife Désirée

Charles Hallé aged 31; after an oil
painting by Victor Mottez

shoulders the blame of the break-down is laid, and most deservedly so; it is, therefore, most unlikely that he should himself try to provoke one. The effect of the 'Requiem', and especially of the 'Tuba mirum', was so overpowering that I have never dared to produce it in England, where it has been my joy to conduct so many of Berlioz's works; the placing of four orchestras at the corners of the principal one is impossible in our concert rooms, and I consider it indispensable for the due effect of the movement and the carrying out of the composer's intention.

Of his perfect command over the orchestra, Berlioz gave an extraordinary proof on the occasion of a grand concert given by him a few years later in the 'Cirque Franconi'. There had been a very long rehearsal in the morning, at which I was present, as I had to play Beethoven's G major concerto, then very seldom performed. After some hours hard work Berlioz dismissed the orchestra; I remained with him, and hardly had the last member of the band vanished when Berlioz struck his forehead, exclaiming: 'I have forgotten the overture!' He stood speechless for a few minutes, then said with determination: 'It *shall* go nevertheless.' Now this overture was the one to 'Le Carnaval Romain', to be performed that evening *for the first time*, and never rehearsed. Musicians who know the work, with its complicated rhythm and all its intricacies, will easily understand how bold the venture was, and will wonder that it could be successful. But to see Berlioz during that performance was a sight never to be forgotten. He watched over every single member of the huge band; his beat was so decisive, his indication of all the *nuances* so clear and so unmistakable, that the overture went smoothly, and no uninitiated person could guess at the absence of a rehearsal.[1] This absolute command over the orchestra I had already admired during the preparations

---

[1] The first performance of *Carnaval Romain* was on February 3, 1844. Berlioz's account of the incident is a little less dramatic: he says that the overture *was* rehearsed, without the wind players.

for the first production of his 'Romeo and Juliet' in 1839, which took a long time, but resulted in a magnificent performance, stirring the public to enthusiasm. His own public I mean; totally distinct from the general one, which did not appreciate or understand his music. Berlioz had at all times a not inconsiderable number of devoted followers, who made up in zeal and admiration for their want of numbers, and to whom he was warmly and somewhat gratefully attached. The indifference shown by the crowd, and even by many musicians, towards his works he felt deeply, although he tried to make light of it, and any real success, however temporary, was eagerly welcomed, and brightened up his life for a while. So the well-known Paganini incident of the previous year had strengthened his courage for a long time, and from a morose made him a most cheerful companion. But thereby hangs a tale which, as all the actors in it are gone to their rest, may be divulged without inconvenience. Armand Bertin, the wealthy and distinguished proprietor of the 'Journal des Débats', had a high regard for Berlioz and knew of all his struggles, which he, Bertin, was anxious to lighten. He resolved therefore to make him a present of 20,000 fr., and in order to enhance the moral effect of this gift he persuaded Paganini to appear as the donor of the money. How well Bertin had judged was proved immediately; what would have been a simple *gracieuseté* from a rich and powerful editor towards one of his staff became a significant tribute from one genius to another, and had a colossal *retentissement*. The secret was well kept and never divulged to Berlioz. It was known, I believe, to but two of Bertin's friends besides myself, one of whom is Mottez, the celebrated painter; I learned it about seven years later when I had become an intimate friend of the house, and Madame Armand Bertin had been for years one of my best pupils.

It was in the year 1840 that I overcame my scruples, and, emerging from my long retirement, gave my first public concert in the Salle Erard Alard and Franchomme assisted

90

me, and the programme opened with Beethoven's trio in B flat. I had hardly played a few bars when I noticed that the pedals had been unhinged and would not act. There was no help for it, and I had to play to the end of the trio without them, after which a few minutes sufficed to set matters right. The consequence of this untoward accident was that all the critics praised me for my judicious and sparing use of the loud pedal, and this reputation clung to me in Paris ever afterwards, although undeservedly so. I was much flattered to see Liszt, Chopin, and Meyerbeer amongst the audience, and felt deeply grateful to them for thus encouraging a young artist on his *début*. The concert was successful, and from that moment my public appearances multiplied, my name became known, and the number of my pupils increased constantly, so that in 1841 I felt justified in marrying, and once more the number 11 became of significance in my life: for I was twice 11 years old, and married on the 11th of the 11th month of the year. My wife, *née* Désirée Smith de Rilieu, was born at New Orleans, and had been residing for some years in Paris with her mother, a widow. Madame Smith had a negro servant, formerly one of her slaves, who had followed her to France, and was much attached to her. It was customary in Paris to give a party, a ball generally, to the friends of the bride and bridegroom on the eve of the wedding, a custom which we followed. Madame Smith's confidential servant had been instructed to engage a number of day-waiters for the occasion, and great was my consternation when at the proper moment the ices were brought in by ten waiters—all grinning niggers!

In the summer of 1842 I made a short concert tour through Germany, playing at Wiesbaden, Mayence, Frankfort, Darmstadt, and other towns. At Frankfort I had the happiness to meet Mendelssohn, and to spend a few weeks closely associated with him and rich in musical delight. At the concert I gave, he and Hiller[1] played with

[1] Ferdinand Hiller (1811-85), pianist and composer.

91

me Bach's triple concerto in D minor, and at Hiller's house, where we usually met, I became acquainted with the Scotch symphony, then unpublished, of which he had just finished the admirable arrangement as a pianoforte duet, which we played over and over again from the manuscript. There I heard also for the first time his 'Variations Sérieuses', and some of the then unpublished 'Lieder ohne Worte', amongst them the now so popular 'Frühlingslied'. Mendelssohn's playing was not exactly that of a 'virtuoso', not to be compared with that of Liszt or Thalberg (he himself called it 'en gros spielen'), but it was remarkably perfect, and one felt the great musician, the great composer, in every bar he played. He was also a great organist, and I had the privilege of hearing him improvise, and also play two of his fine organ sonatas. The greatest treat, however, was to sit with him at the piano and listen to innumerable fragments from half-forgotten beautiful works by Cherubini, Gluck, Bach, Palestrina, Marcello, 'tutti quanti'. It was only enough to mention one of them, whether it was a Gloria from one of Cherubini's Masses or a psalm by Marcello, to hear it played to perfection, until I came to the conclusion that he knew every bar of music ever written, and, what was more, could reproduce it immediately. One morning Hiller and I were playing together one of Bach's organ pieces on the piano, one of no particular interest, but which we wished to know better. When we were in the middle of it, a part hardly to be distinguished from many other similar ones, the door opened, Mendelssohn entered, and, without interrupting us, rose on tip-toes, and with his up-lifted finger pointed significantly at the next bar which was coming and contained an unexpected and striking modulation. So from hearing through the door a bar or two of a—for Bach— somewhat commonplace piece, he not only recognised it at once, but knew the exact place we had arrived at, and what was to follow in the next bar, a most surprising proof of intimate knowledge. His memory was indeed prodigious.

It is well known that when he revived Bach's 'Passion Music', and conducted the first performance of that immortal work after it had been dormant for about a century, he found, stepping to the conductor's desk, that a score similar in binding and thickness, but of another work, had been brought by mistake. He conducted this amazingly complicated work by heart, turning leaf after leaf of the book he had before him, in order not to create any feeling of uneasiness on the part of the executants.[1]

Mendelssohn, and certainly Berlioz, would have been amazed if they had witnessed the modern craze for conducting without the score; *they* never did so, even with their own works, which certainly they must have known better than anybody else. There can be no possible advantage in dispensing with the score, a glance at which shows to the conductor the whole instrumentation, and enables him to watch over every detail of the execution, and over the entries of the most secondary instruments. No conductor could write by heart twenty pages of the full score of a symphony, or other work, exactly with the instrumentation of the composer (perhaps the composer himself could not do it); he must therefore remain ignorant whilst conducting, of what the minor instruments, say the second clarinet, second bassoon, second flute, and many others, have to do—a serious disadvantage. The public who go into ecstasies over 'conducting by heart' do not know how very easy it is, how much easier, for instance, than playing a concerto or a sonata by heart, at which nobody wonders. Without the score the conductor has only to be acquainted with the general outline of the composition and its salient features; then, the better the band the easier the task of its chief.

But to return to Frankfort. The few weeks spent there in the intimacy of Mendelssohn and Hiller are amongst the most precious, the most interesting, I have ever lived, and

[1] This historic *St Matthew Passion* was given in Berlin on March 11, 1829.

are engraved in my memory with a point of gold. I never met Mendelssohn again. On a renewed visit to Frankfort in the autumn of 1843 I received an invitation to play at Darmstadt before the Grand Duke of Hesse, and I was delighted to see my dear old master, Rinck, again on the same occasion. Coming to the castle on the appointed evening I was ushered into the still untenanted music room, where after a time I was joined by a gentleman in simple evening dress who entertained me most politely, telling me that the Grand Ducal party, which included the Grand Duke of Saxe-Weimar, would soon appear. I took my informant for one of the gentlemen of the Court, and as he was so very amiable I asked him to be kind enough to point out to me the different distinguished personages, who, I said, would probably be familiar to him by sight, but were not so to me. He promised most willingly to do so, and it gave me rather a start when I found half-an-hour later that my kind *cicerone* was the celebrated Prince Alexander of Hesse. The party was a small one, and listened to my performance with a willing ear. What has impressed the evening upon my memory is the circumstance that while I was playing, a despatch was brought in announcing the birth of a son to the Crown Princess of Russia (a Princess of Hesse Darmstadt), which caused such joy that the two Grand Dukes not only embraced, but in spite of their bulky persons, which hardly permitted their short arms to reach each other, waltzed together through the long and almost empty room. It was a touching but curious spectacle. After half an hour's interruption I was allowed to continue my performance. The next day I had the honour of being received by Prince Alexander at his own villa, and could explain my *bévue* of the previous evening.

During the few months my wife and I spent in Germany, having before our departure given notice to quit the rooms in the Rue de l'Arcade, in Paris, with which we were dissatisfied, a cousin of my wife's, the Comtesse de

Rochefort, proposed we should take the rooms which she occupied in the Rue Blanche, as she was leaving for the south of France. I had been often at her evening parties, knew the rooms perfectly, which were most convenient, and we struck the bargain at once. Great was my consternation when, on arriving in September at these much coveted rooms, I found that the building opposite was the Gymnase Musical Militaire, from which nearly all the regimental bands were recruited, and in which hundreds of young men practised the whole day long with open windows, weather permitting, all the wind instruments ever invented, all at the same time, every man in his own key, and doing his own exercises. No more infernal noise can be imagined and I was in despair, but I had signed a short lease and we were obliged to remain where we were; and such is the force of habit, that after a few months I was no longer disturbed by the abominable neighbourhood, and could even give my lessons in peace.

There was one thing, however, which was impossible, viz., to have musical afternoons on Sundays. Our friends could not have enjoyed them, for Sunday was no day of rest for the poor 'piou-pious' opposite; they had to practise till six in the evening as on week-days. I therefore ventured to call upon the director of the Gymnase, the whilom celebrated Italian composer, Carafa, stated my case to him, and induced him, not without trouble, on a certain number of Sundays during the season to stop all practice from three o'clock in the afternoon, much to the relief of the overworked pupils, who were always anxious to give me proofs of their gratitude. Indeed, once, when a fire had broken out in our kitchen, they swarmed into the house, extinguished it, and in their zeal did much more mischief than the fire could have done. These musical afternoons became gradually more and more important, and it was there that, timidly at first, I tried to win acceptance for some of Beethoven's pianoforte works; for, with the exception of two trios, the Kreutzer and the so-called

'Moonlight' sonata, none were known to other than a few earnest students. A great attraction was the exquisite singing, or rather declaiming, of Delsarte, a most extraordinary artist whose dramatic power I have never heard equalled. His voice was far from fine, being rather disagreeable, but it was immediately forgotten after the first few notes, and he held his hearers spellbound. I shall never forget the impression he created when singing Gluck's beautiful air: 'Cruelle, non, jamais ton coeur ne fut touché par mes alarmes.' It was indescribable. Every syllable told, and the accents of despair were irresistible and inimitable. He sang at nearly every one of my matinées, for which I owe him a debt of gratitude. Lamartine, Odillon Barrot, Ledru Rollin, and Salvandy, who heard him at my house, each one complimented him in the same words: 'Monsieur, vous êtes un grand orateur,' of which he complained to me with perhaps pardonable pride by saying, 'These gentlemen think there is nothing above an orator.' Delsarte died in a monastery, for which, at the time I knew him intimately, he certainly seemed to have no vocation.

My life at this time became one of uninterrupted intellectual enjoyment, which will be easily understood by my readers when I enumerate a few of the names of distinguished men, in the most various walks of life, whom I could call personal friends: Ary Scheffer, Lamartine, Salvandy, Ledru Rollin, Alexandre Dumas *père,* Ingres, Meyerbeer, Halévy, Delacroix, Louis Blanc, Guizot, 'Maître' Marie, not to forget Berlioz, Heller, Heine, Ernst, Jules Janin, Liszt, Chopin, and a host of others equally remarkable.[1] Paris was then in reality what Wagner wished to make Bayreuth, the centre of civilisation; and such a galaxy of celebrities as it contained has, I believe, never

---

[1] Odillon Barrot, Alexandre-Auguste Ledru-Rollin and Louis Blanc were reformist politicians of 1848. The historian François Guizot was the minister whose administration fell in 1848. Jules Janin held long sway as dramatic critic for the influential *Journal des Débats.*

been assembled again. The charm of Parisian life at that period was that in certain 'salons', on fixed evenings in the week, most of these 'mighty ones' were to be met.

Such a 'salon' was that of Armand Bertin, made delightful as much by the charm of his wife as by his own intellectual power. It was there that I often met M. Ingres, and had the honour of playing some of Mozart's violin sonatas with him. Great artist as he was, with an immense reputation, he thought less of his painting than of his violin playing, which, to say the least of it, was vile. He generally was so moved by any Andante we played together, that he shed copious tears, and he drew them also from the eyes of his listeners, but they were not tears of delight. His immense superiority as an artist made this little weakness very interesting. An amusing incident occurred when, after his return from Rome, where he had been for years the director of the French 'Académie', a grand dinner was given him, as a welcome, in the Salle Ventadour, at which every notability in Paris was present. After the speech in his honour, pronounced by whom I cannot remember, and received with uproarious enthusiasm, Ingres rose and returned thanks, and after wiping his spectacles, wet with tears as usual, he drew a paper from his pocket, adjusted it to the light, and the first words he read were: 'Les acclamations que je viens d'entendre.' It seemed odd and 'naïf' that the words should have been written before the cheers were heard.

Ingres was passionately fond of music—a passion shared by nearly all the great painters with whom I have come in contact—while amongst poets and literary men the devotees to music seem to form an exception. Ary Scheffer, the noble painter whose fame was at its zenith in the forties, was never happier than when listening to music; hence his friendship with Chopin, Liszt, and a select number of musicians amongst whom I was happy to hold a place. To play to him in his studio, whilst he was engaged upon one of his great canvases, was one of my greatest delights.

The well-known picture of 'Christ tempted by Satan' (Liszt sitting as a model for Satan) was commenced and finished with the accompaniment of my music. Scheffer's works no longer hold the position in the world of art which they held at that time—a time when they were sought for, in England especially, with avidity; he knew this, and on one occasion, speaking of this popularity, he added musingly, after a moment's silence, 'Cela me donne à penser.'

In 1843 I made my first acquaintance with England, a very unsatisfactory one as it proved. Unannounced, I came over in the middle of the season on the invitation, principally, of one English friend, Mr. Fitzherbert, whom I had known for years in Paris. My name was not sufficiently known to open the doors of the big institutions to me at once; still, I received an invitation from the directors of the Philharmonic Society to play at their last concert, but coupled with the condition that I should perform a concerto by Griffin, one of the directors. This I declined, and consequently did not play at all. I took part in a concert given by Sivori, and gave a concert in the Hanover Square rooms, at which Clara Novello and Balfe sang, and Sivori played, but the success of which was indifferent. So, after a sojourn of about eight weeks I returned to Paris, firmly resolved to shun England for ever! The short season had, however, not been altogether uninteresting to me, enlivened as it was by a dispute between Ernst and Sivori on the subject of the authorship of 'Le Carnaval de Venise'. I was charmed to meet Sivori in London, having made his acquaintance in the previous year, and fully recognised his claims to distinction, in spite of the pompous title 'only pupil of Paganini,' which he assumed. I was often with him and glad of his society, when a few weeks later Ernst arrived. He was fresh from a triumphant tour through Holland and Belgium, and his coming was expected with much curiosity. Ernst was an older friend of mine than Sivori, as a musician he was far his superior, our tastes were more similar, and I naturally continued those friendly relations with him which had so long been my wont. I did not mean to neglect Sivori, but found to my surprise and sorrow that he looked upon my conduct with regard to Ernst as upon the worst of all betrayals. He had fully expected that I should *cut* Ernst, whom he considered his rival, and could not understand how I could dream of being friends with both sides. I had indeed dreamed of bringing them together, which would have been a pleasure to Ernst; but when I hinted at this, the ire of Sivori knew no bounds, and I had to make a selection between the two, much against my will, but of course in favour of my old friend. Ernst achieved a great success and a well deserved one, for his talent was at its very height and his passionate playing most impressive. I rejoiced at his triumph all the more, as for a short time I had harboured serious doubts on the subject, prompted by a curious and somewhat ludicrous scene which I had witnessed a few days after his arrival.

The directors of the Philharmonic Society had decided upon fêting Ernst on his arrival and arranged a party at Richmond in his honour, which took the shape of an early dinner. The day was very fine, the company, including the principal critics, very numerous, and the dinner sumptuous. Ernst had to respond to many civilities, to empty his glass at the separate request of each of the 'convives', so often that at last I saw that he was overcome, and feared that he might roll under the table. It was at that critical moment that somebody proposed Ernst should play something. The proposal was cheered vociferously, and as Ernst's violin did not dine out, some one was despatched into the village to try and find one. He soon returned with a violin, the price of which, with the bow, was marked fifteen shillings. This was handed to Ernst, and he gave the very first proof of his talent to a select English audience by playing his arrangement of Schubert's 'Erl King', for violin alone, an impossible piece, which in his best days he could not play satisfactorily. Upon this wretched instrument and in a more than half-tipsy condition, it was excruciating, and I gave him up for lost; but, whether it was that his listeners were in the same state as he, or that the extraordinary sounds they heard bewildered them, his triumph was complete! What is more, after his great and legitimate success, at a concert given on July 18 in aid of the German Hospital, his first public appearance in London, I heard it said with conviction, 'Ah, but his playing at Richmond was even finer!' The party was further enlivened by poor half-blind George Macfarren running straight into the Thames and having to be fished out, fortunately without any hurt to him.

I had brought a few letters of introduction with me, one of which was to a most amiable man, a member of Parliament, who a few years later rose to a high position in the Government. . . . I had left the letter at his house with my card, and he called upon me the very next day, was charming, most kind, and to my great satisfaction spoke French most fluently. He knew from the letter it was my wish to be heard, and as it so happened that he had a large evening party two days later, he proposed that I should play a few pieces during the evening, saying that I should meet many influential people, with whom I would certainly be glad to make acquaintance. I accepted readily. When he withdrew he turned back at the door and said, 'Might I ask you in what style you play?' I was puzzled and could not give a clear answer. He next asked, 'Do you know Mr. Alexander Dreyschock?' 'Yes,' I said, 'he is an admirable and powerful pianist.' 'Do you play in his style?' 'No, I can conscientiously say that my style differs from his.' 'Oh, I am so glad,' said my friend, 'for he plays so loud, *et cela impêche les dames de causer.*' I meekly suggested that no music at all might perhaps be more to the purpose, but he would not hear of that, insisted upon my coming, and I did go, played two pieces, and can give myself credit for not having *empêché les dames de causer,* nor the gentlemen either.

This shows in what estimation music was held in 1843 in the most fashionable society; the change that has taken place since then is astounding.

Another of my letters of introduction was to Count d'Orsay, the brilliant and eccentric *roi des modes*. I drove to Kensington Gore, where he lived, and after ringing the bell at the gate, a small side door opened to give passage to the head of the porter who inquired my business. I told him I had a letter to deliver to Count d'Orsay, and at his request gave it to him, together with my card. He then shut the door, leaving me wondering in the street. About ten minutes later the door opened again, I was admitted and conducted through a long avenue to the luxurious house, in which the Count received me with the utmost politeness and grace. When after half an hour I took my departure, he begged me to renew my visit and to excuse him if he did not return my call, as for various reasons he did not go out much. It then dawned upon me that if he ventured out he might possibly not re-enter the house for a long time, and that for this reason such precautions were used in admitting unknown visitors. I was afterwards invited to several small evening parties at Gore House, made delightful by Lady Blessington's grace and d'Orsay's wit. Prince Napoleon was generally one of the guests, but at that time only interested me by his historical name, and I cannot recollect anything characteristic connected with him. In July I returned to Paris with Ernst, little satisfied with England, and much less anticipating that it would eventually become my home, my cherished home.

Nothing of importance happened during the rest of the year, and the circle of my acquaintance extended further and further, the number of my pupils increased steadily, and I had every reason to be satisfied with my lot. My ambition, however, was not entirely satisfied, for, although successful at my own and many other concerts, I had not been invited to play at the 'Concerts du Conservatoire', which then, even more than at present, was the highest distinction to which an artist could aspire. I did not venture to claim the honour for fear of a refusal, which would have pained me. One evening, returning on foot from a late party, as I was passing Rue Taitbout I sang tolerably loud, there being no one very near, the theme of the Finale of Beethoven's Choral Symphony, which I had heard on the previous Sunday at the Conservatoire. I had not noticed a gentleman who was walking about five yards before me in the same direction, and who, hearing me sing, stopped when I came up to him, when I recognised the redoubtable conductor of the 'Concerts du Conservatoire', M. Habeneck, whose personal acquaintance I had not made. He addressed me with, 'Ah, vous chantez la Neuvième?' and on my replying with a few enthusiastic expressions, he asked brusquely: 'Who are you?' I gave my name, upon which he shook hands with me, said he had heard often of my doings, and to my surprise and delight ended with the question: 'Why don't you play at our concerts?' I explained frankly that I had not dared to apply for such an honour; and 'Call to-morrow and we will arrange that,' was his welcome answer. And so I played at the Conservatoire most unexpectedly in 1844, and had every reason to be satisfied with the reception that was accorded to me. I had chosen Beethoven's E flat concerto, my interpretation of which met with almost general approval. I say 'almost' because after the performance a much respected member of the orchestra, Urhan, the principal viola, apostrophised me with: 'Why do you change Beethoven?' I had not really *changed* anything in the text, but, misled by the example of Liszt, I used then for the sake of effect to play some passages in octaves instead of in single notes, and otherwise amplify certain passages. This Urhan did not like, and his rebuke was well merited. I think Liszt must have felt equal scruples, for when, on the occasion of the unveiling of Beethoven's statue at Bonn in August, 1845, he played the same concerto, he adhered scrupulously to the text, and a finer and grander reading of the work could not be

imagined. Urhan was a remarkable viola player, the best I
ever heard, and a singular character, very outspoken, as his
remark to me proves, and one of the most upright men that
ever lived. He was of an extremely religious turn of mind,
and accepted the position of principal viola at the Grand
Opera, which he held for a long term of years, only on the
condition that his seat was to be so arranged that he might
turn his back upon the stage and avoid witnessing the
abominations of the ballet. The Beethoven festival at
Bonn, mentioned incidentally just now, to which Berlioz
and I journeyed together from Paris, drew together a large
number of the most notable musicians from all countries,
all anxious to do homage to the memory of that incomparable genius. It was graced by the presence of the King of
Prussia and his guests, Queen Victoria and the Prince
Consort, who witnessed from a royal box built purposely in
the square the unveiling of the statue, which, to the astonishment of the multitude that surrounded it, was found
when the veil fell to turn its back upon the Royalties.

Liszt was the hero of the fête, and justly so, for without
his colossal exertions it would never have taken place. He
was seldom to be approached by us, so great was the crowd
of his admirers that besieged him constantly; but the
occasional half hours that he could spare to Berlioz and
myself were made memorable by the flashes of his
eloquence and his wit. His speech was indeed golden. At
the first concert he played us, however, an unpardonable
trick. For the opening of the programme he had composed
a cantata of considerable length, devoid of interest, as the
rehearsals had shown us, but which we had resigned ourselves to listen to patiently, and so we did.[1] Hardly was it
concluded, and we were preparing ourselves to enjoy
Beethoven's music, when the Royalties, who had been
detained until then, entered their box, and Liszt, to our
dismay, began the whole cantata over again, inflicting it a

---

[1] *Zur Säcular-Feier Beethovens* for soloists, chorus and orchestra.

second time on the immense audience, who, out of respect for the crowned heads, had to endure it, though probably not without inward grumbling. One morning, during this week of festivities, I found him alone, and the conversation turning upon events and anecdotes which had made the years from 1838 to 1846 memorable to both of us, he suddenly exclaimed, 'Ah, l'heureux temps! où l'on pouvait être si bête!' He spoke feelingly, and I think rendered himself justice, for the things he could say and do during that period when he was the best fêted artist that perhaps had ever lived bordered really on the ludicrous. Thus, after his great triumphs in Germany, especially in Berlin, where the ladies had fought for his gloves, I heard him say at one of his receptions in Paris, the name of the King of Prussia being mentioned: 'Le roi a été très *convenable!*' To be different from the rest of mankind, to know nothing of the usual modes of living, or rather to appear ignorant of them, seemed his one aim. Once, having accidentally met me on the Boulevards, he asked me to dine with him at the Café de Paris. We enjoyed a good but simple dinner, and when the waiter brought him the bill, which could hardly have amounted to 30 frs., he asked me quite seriously if I thought 40 frs. for the waiter would be sufficient! 'Je ne sais jamais ces choses,' he said, and without my remonstrances he would have given to the waiter more than the whole dinner had cost. Calling upon him one day I found him engaged with his tailor, and busy looking at patterns for waistcoats. 'I have at least sixty,' said he to me, 'but never find one to my liking when I want it.' 'What do you say to this pattern?' he asked presently, and on my approving of it he came out with 'Voulez-vous que je vous en fasse faire un?'—a kind offer which was declined with thanks.

One scene I witnessed characterises another side of his behaviour at that time. The programme of one of his concerts given in the 'Salle du Conservatoire' contained the 'Kreutzer' sonata to be played by Liszt and Massart, a celebrated and much esteemed violinist, professor at the

Conservatoire. Massart was just commencing the first bar of the introduction when a voice from the audience called out 'Robert le Diable!' At that time Liszt had composed a very brilliant fantasia on themes from that opera, and played it always with immense success. The call was taken up by other voices, and in a moment the cries 'Robert le Diable!' 'Robert le Diable!' drowned the tones of the violin. Liszt rose, bowed, and said: 'Je suis toujours l'humble serviteur du public, mais est-ce qu'on désire la fantaisie avant ou après la sonate?' Renewed cries of 'Robert, Robert!' were the answer, upon which Liszt turned half round to poor Massart and dismissed him with a wave of the hand, without a syllable of excuse or regret. He did play the fantasia magnificently, rousing the public to a frenzy of enthusiasm, then called Massart out of his retreat, and we had the 'Kreutzer', which somehow no longer seemed in its right place. On another occasion, at a concert given for the benefit of the Polish refugees at the house of Princess Czartoriska, he did me the honour to ask me to play a duet for two pianos with him, and chose Thalberg's well-known 'Fantasia' on 'Norma'. We had no rehearsal, but he said to me: 'Let us take the theme of the variations at a moderate pace, the effect will be better.' Now the first part of this theme is accompanied on the second piano (which Liszt had chosen) by octaves for both hands, which octaves in the second part fall to the lot of the first piano. What was my horror when, in spite of the caution he had given me, Liszt started his octaves at such a pace that I did not conceive the possibility of getting through my portion of them alive. Somehow I managed it, badly enough, but if I ever understood the French saying 'suer sang et eau' it was then. I had my revenge, however. In the second variation, where the pianos successively accompany the theme with chromatic scales, Liszt, instead of confining himself to the scales, altered them by introducing double and additional notes, a feat of amazing difficulty, which made my hair stand on end, but which I did not feel compelled to try and

105

imitate, simple chromatic scales neatly and rapidly played being, on the whole, more effective; so when my turn came I confined myself to them, and earned a round of applause in which Liszt most generously joined.

Of his ready wit the following little anecdote, hardly known I believe, may serve as an example. A choral society of amateurs had been formed in Paris under his direction, most of the members belonging to the highest aristocracy. At the rehearsals Princess Belgiojoso, an accomplished musician, accompanied on the piano. As an accompanist she had, however, serious faults, for she took great liberties with the time, treating what she had to play as if it had been a 'Nocturne' or 'Ballade' by Chopin, her admired master. During one of these rehearsals, at which I was present by invitation, a young German tenor, not perfectly at home in the French tongue, complained of these liberties by muttering in a low voice at first, but which grew louder and louder: 'Il n'y a pas de *tact*, il n'y a pas de *tact*,' evidently under the impression that the German word 'takt' had the same meaning in French. After a while Liszt corrected him by saying: 'Monsieur, Madame la Princesse manque de *mesure*, mais *vous* manquez de *tact*.'

Of the years between 1843 and 1847 it only remains to relate that in 1843 I had the honour of being commanded to play at the Château d'Eu on the occasion of the visit of H.M. Queen Victoria and Prince Albert to Louis Philippe. The orchestra and chorus of the Conservatoire had also been summoned, and Auber was director of the music in general. On the entrance, on Louis Philippe's arm, of Queen Victoria into the music-room, she was most appropriately greeted with the beautiful chorus from Gluck's 'Iphigénie en Aulide', commencing 'Que de grâce, que de majesté.' Those were brilliant days, favoured by the most beautiful weather. One incident connected with my trip to Eu was very original. I learnt, one day before the concert at which I was to play, that there was no piano at the château fit to be used on such an occasion, and I had to send one from Paris. But how to send it? That was the question. There was not time for the usual mode of conveyance, so I went to the office of the diligence, where the mention of a grand piano by Erard as part of my luggage was at first received with derisive laughter. But the magical words 'Par ordre du roi' overcame the difficulty, and the piano was stowed on the top of the huge diligence, the only instance on record, I believe, of a pianist travelling in the same carriage with his instrument.

The year 1847 forms an epoch in my musical life. I had then long been prominently before the public, and felt strong enough to venture upon the institution of a series of 'concerts de musique de chambre', never before tried in Paris. In Alard and Franchomme, the two foremost performers on the violin and violoncello, admirable artists both, I found willing, even enthusiastic, colleagues. The 'Salle du Conservatoire' was granted us, and in February 1847 we gave our first concert, before an audience which included the very *élite* of Parisian artistic and literary society. Lamartine, Georges Sand, Horace Vernet, Ary Scheffer, Guizot, Salvandy, Ledru Rollin, Marie, Alexandre Dumas, and many others equally celebrated, filled the boxes as subscribers. I was well aware of the progress the taste for good music had made during the last decade. Still, the success of these concerts, purely instrumental ones, surpassed my most sanguine expectations. Soon it became almost as difficult to obtain tickets for them as for the great concerts of the Conservatoire; in fact, we scored a great success. The programmes consisted exclusively of *ensemble* music, from duets to quintets, Armingand holding the post of second violin, and Casimir Nery that of viola. The preparation for the concerts was a labour of love for us all, and rehearsals took place every day while the series lasted. It seems strange to me now, writing in 1895, that so many universally-known works like Mendelssohn's trios, Schumann's quintet and quartet, had then the charm of absolute novelty. This first season having been so eminently successful, the announcement of the second in 1848 drew together a still greater number of subscribers, so that every place was disposed of before the first concert, which took place at the commencement of February.

Two concerts had been given when the Revolution broke out, and to me everything was changed as by magic. In Paris by far the greatest part of a musician's income was invariably derived from teaching; so it was with Chopin, Heller, many others, and myself; but from the day after the Revolution the pupils disappeared, and at the end of a week I could only boast of one (he was an old Englishman), and my friends Alard and Franchomme had none left. The audience at our third concert did not number fifty people, although every place was subscribed for. The outlook was most gloomy and I realised soon that a serious crisis had arrived in my life, and that an immediate determination had to be taken for the sake of my family, which consisted then of my wife and two small children. What determination it was to be I could not at once decide, but I felt that I must be free, and resolved therefore to abandon the remaining five concerts of the series, my colleagues concurring readily. We announced that the money would be returned, and on the very day that the announcement appeared my house was literally besieged from morning to evening by eager applicants, money being for a while so scarce that daily processions of people were seen going to the mint to exchange their silver valuables for ready cash.

Of the Revolution itself I can only relate what I saw with my own eyes, and that is very little, although at one moment my life was in danger, viz. on the eve of the Revolution, when nothing serious was expected. I had gone with a friend (M. Guibert) to look at the crowds on the Boulevards, and found that the Foreign Office on the Boulevard des Capucines was guarded by a *carré* of military, which obliged us to pass through the Rue Basse des

Remparts, having the soldiers some 10 or 12 feet above our heads. This street was densely crowded and we advanced very slowly, when suddenly, without any warning, we were fired into with terrible effect, a woman close by my side and a child within my reach being both shot dead. The surprise was dreadful, and Boulevard and street were cleared in an instant. I reached my house without accident, meeting only flying people, and intensely enjoyed the feeling of safety. We lived then at the corner of the Place St. Georges, a circular place into which four streets lead. The next morning, between five and six o'clock, I was awakened by a singular noise under our windows, and, stepping upon the balcony, I saw that the four streets had been barricaded and that all communication between the Place St. Georges and the rest of the world had been cut off. The barricades were manned by a set of ill-looking, hirsute people, armed with antediluvian weapons. The construction of the barricades not being finished yet, the mob paid small attention to the inhabitants of the houses that surrounded the Place. A little later, however, when stepping a second time on to the balcony, I saw Madame Thiers come out of her house in a loose dressing-gown, carrying several guns and handing them to the insurgents, with whom M. Thiers, as leader of the Opposition and credited with Republican tendencies, stood in high favour. As I had the advantage of a slight acquaintance with M. and Mme. Thiers, whose house was the second from the one in which I lived with my family, I descended quickly and approached her, to compare notes, not a little pleased to put myself apparently under her protection and thereby to gain some respect from our ruffian captors. But there was little to fear from them, as it proved. They asked for arms, of which I had none to give, and for wine, which they drank 'on the premises', but without excess. The flags on the barricades bore on the first day the inscription, 'Vive la Réforme', which was changed the next day into 'Vive la République'. Being pretty far from the centre of Paris, we heard no news,

109

everything seemed quiet, and only twice during the day did we see a regiment of soldiers pass through the Rue St. Lazare, at the end of our street, with their guns reversed, from which we concluded that at all events part of the army had fraternised with the people. Our friends of the barricades cheered them most vociferously, but had no more news of what was going on than we.

On the evening of the second day this imprisonment became intolerable to me, and I ventured to ask the sentinels if I might go to inquire after my friends. Permission being given, I passed through and found a second barricade at the end of the street, which also proved no obstacle. Fortunately, I found my friends, of whom Heller was the first I visited, all well, heard for the first time of the flight of Louis Philippe, the formation of a 'Gouvernement provisoire', and after an hour's absence returned home with this weighty news. Approaching the lower barricade of our street, I was challenged by a most ferocious-looking individual in the gruffest of voices with 'Qui vive?' I drew as near to him as I could and said that I really did not know under the circumstances what was the proper answer to give, but that I only wanted to return to my family in the Place St. Georges, which I had left but an hour before. Apparently satisfied, he screamed out, looking more grim than before, 'Eh bien, passez! mais prenez garde là-bas!' Alarmed and thinking of possible ambuscades, I asked him what danger threatened me 'là-bas.' 'C'est qu'il y a de l'eau,' was the answer. It had been raining, and the pavement having been partially taken up, there were pools of water here and there, and my formidable-looking challenger was anxious that I should not wet my feet! A rose-coloured revolution, indeed! One, however, which completely destroyed my prospects in Paris and forced me to consider very seriously what to do next. I could not remain in Paris, and my thoughts began to travel towards London, when one day M. de Soligny, formerly French Chargé d'Affaires in Mexico, called with a message from

M. de Lamartine, the chief of the 'Gouvernement provisoire'. The message was nothing less than the offer of the secretaryship at the French Embassy to the German Diet in Frankfort, Soligny being the chosen ambassador. I believe, however, that he never occupied the post. Twenty-four hours were given me for my decision, and those were most anxious hours, but at the end of them I felt that musician I was and musician I must remain. I declined the tempting offer, and went direct to Lamartine to express my thanks and to explain my reasons for refusing it. A fortnight more was spent in consultation with my best friends, the result of which was that I decided upon going to London, there to seek a new existence for my family.

I left Paris in March 1848 with a very heavy heart indeed; not only had I to leave my family behind me at first, but the separation from so many friends, from a society which I had good reason to think unequalled in the world, was a hard wrench. Often during my twelve years of residence there had I said to myself that it would be impossible for me to live anywhere else, and now I had to say 'adieu' most unexpectedly; for, one short month before, I thought myself secure in Paris for the rest of my lifetime. A new life was to begin for me in England; but before I narrate what befell me here, I must throw a few retrospective glances upon people I met in Paris and who have not yet been mentioned in these memoirs.

Place aux dames. In my earliest recollection dwells one evening in 1839, when a friend took me to one of the receptions of Mademoiselle Taglioni, the celebrated dancer, the admired of the admired, whose every attitude, every motion, was an embodiment of grace, a study for the sculptor and painter. My admiration for her knew no bounds, and to be in her own salon was great happiness to me. There were crowds of people there, and the best names of France were represented: my excitement was intense when she kindly asked me to play something. I did so, and then behind my back I heard her say to a friend, 'mais il

111

joue comme un ange'; words that thrilled my every nerve. I could not approach her again during the evening, and the next time I met her was about forty years later, when at a dinner-party in London I found myself seated by her side. Then I told her of that, to me, memorable evening, repeated to her the very words she had spoken, never forgotten by me, and added: 'Ah, Madame Taglioni, if you knew how deeply in love I was with you at that time!' 'Et vous me dites cela maintenant!' was her prompt reply.

Another remarkable lady, very different from Mademoiselle Taglioni, for she was a confirmed invalid, was Mademoiselle Louisa Bertin, sister of Armand Bertin, spoken of in Parisian society invariably as Mademoiselle Louisa, just as if she had been some royalty. She was a most distinguished lady, and a very clever and serious musician, accomplishing even the composition of an opera, 'Esmeralda', which, through the influence of the 'Journal des Débats', was actually performed at the Grand Opéra, called then 'L'Académie Royale de Musique'. The work had no success, and was withdrawn after a few performances. What I remember best was the general rehearsal, when the stalls were crowded with celebrities of all kinds: friends of the autocrat Armand, and also of the very amiable lady whose work they were invited to judge. Rossini was placed on the stage in an easy chair close to the scenery on the left side, and was, of course, the observed of all observers. He gave no sign during the first act, but in the middle of the second, when a momentary pause had occurred, he rose and advanced slowly towards the conductor. Immediately a whisper ran through the whole house—'Rossini va parler'—everybody was all ears, and this was what he said: 'Monsieur Habeneck, vous ne voyez donc pas? Il y a un quinquet qui fume'; and he returned to his seat. A somewhat similar scene, of which, however, I was not an eye-witness, had occurred at one of the rehearsals of his own 'Guillaume Tell'. There, also, during a pause, he had crossed the stage up to a spot from which he could speak to M. Brod, the celebrated oboe player, professor of the Conservatoire, whom he addressed with, 'M. Brod, have you your snuff-box with you?' 'Yes, maestro.' 'Then give me a pinch.' The pinch duly taken, he continued: 'M. Brod, in the introduction to such and such an air there occurs an F which you play sharp; I should prefer it natural, if you please. With regard to the F sharp, *ne vous en tourmentez pas: nous trouverons moyen de la placer ailleurs.*' I had occasion to relate this little anecdote to Berlioz, who jumped up from his chair, exclaiming, 'C'est foudroyant d'esprit!'

A remarkable man I met now and then at the house of M. Mallet in 1840 and 1841 was Donizetti, a most distinguished, amiable, and fashionable gentleman, as elegant as most of his music. He was young still, but such a prolific composer that at that time he had already written upwards of forty operas. I remember talking with him about Rossini, and asking if Rossini had really composed the 'Barbiere' in a fortnight. 'Oh, I quite believe it,' said he, 'he has always been such a lazy fellow!' I confess that I looked with wonder and admiration at a man who considered that to spend a whole fortnight over the composition of an opera was a waste of time. Another and much more remarkable man, whom I saw several times at my friend Leo's house, was Alexander von Humboldt,[1] certainly the most celebrated man of his time. When the invitation bore the words 'To meet Humboldt', the rooms were naturally crowded, and he was the cynosure of all eyes. Wherever he stood a crowd of eager listeners assembled around him, all mute and full of reverence, and intent on every word that fell from his lips. He never attempted to lead or originate a conversation in the true sense of the word; he always spoke alone, delivering a lecture on one subject or another, and was never anxious to hear anybody else's opinion. I was once asked to play for him, and looked upon this invita-

---

[1] Naturalist, explorer and founder of modern physical geography.

tion as an event in my life. There had been a momentary silence in the rooms, but the moment I began to play von Humboldt began to hold forth on a new and evidently most interesting topic, his voice rising with every one of my *crescendos,* dominating my most powerful *fortes,* and resuming its normal level only with my most delicate phrases. It was a duet which I did not sustain long—'je pliais bagage,' and left the 'champ de bataille' to him, undoubtedly much to the advantage of those whom he addressed.

4

Manchester, 1848-60

With letters and diary extracts

WITH my arrival in March 1848 begins a new epoch in my life, by far the most important and active one, which in many respects has been full of surprises to me. Very far indeed was I then from anticipating that I should one day feel thoroughly at home in England, be proud to become one of her citizens, and play a humble but not altogether unimportant part in the development of her musical taste. My first call was upon my friend Berlioz, who was in trouble through the bankruptcy of Monsieur Jullien,[1] by whom he had been engaged to conduct the opera at Drury Lane. I did not meet him, but returning home from a long round of calls I found the following characteristic note:

Dear Hallé,[2]—I am very *sorry* to have the pleasure of seeing you, nevertheless I thank you for having come to this house so soon after your shipwreck on the coast of England. If you are at home to-night we shall lament together while *smoking.* I shall come to you about ten o'clock. Ever yours,

Hector Berlioz

[1] Louis Jullien (1812-60) was a conductor and impresario with a penchant for publicity. Despite his obvious charlatanry he introduced good music to thousands at his promenade concerts, but is more likely to be remembered for his Monster Quadrille and other eccentricities.

[2] Translation.

And we did ['lament'] together, the future looking very black indeed. The five years which had elapsed since I left London in '43 had, however, brought some change in my position as an artist, and, instead of having to solicit engagements, the opportunity of playing in public was offered to me spontaneously. Some grand orchestral concerts were given at Covent Garden under the direction of Signor Costa, and I soon received an invitation to play Beethoven's E flat concerto at one of them. This I may consider my first public appearance in England, and it was favourably received and criticised. An invitation to play at the Musical Union followed immediately, and was renewed several times during the season. The Musical Union, the predecessor of the Popular Concerts, was originated and directed by Mr. John Ella, and, at the time I speak of, was very flourishing, and the most important concert institution (for chamber music) in London. The Duke of Cambridge was president, and there was a committee composed of members of the highest aristocracy, who, however, did not interfere with the management of the concerts. That was entirely in the hands of Mr. Ella.

Before relating what passed between Mr. Ella and me on the occasion of my first performance at the Musical Union, I must remind my readers that I speak of the year 1848, since which time such a revolution in musical matters has taken place, that what happened then may seem incredible now. When Mr. Ella asked me what I wished to play, and heard that it was one of Beethoven's pianoforte sonatas, he exclaimed, 'Impossible!' and endeavoured to demonstrate that they were not works to be played in public; that, as far as he knew, no solo sonata had ever before been included in any concert programme, and that he could not venture upon offering one to his subscribers. I had to battle for several days before he gave way. He consented at last, and was then much surprised to find that the sonata I had chosen (Op. 31, No. 3 in E flat) pleased so much that several ladies who heard it arranged afternoon parties in order to hear it once more. I have searched the columns of the 'Musical World' for at least fifteen years previous to 1848, but have not found one instance of a sonata being included in a concert programme; Ella therefore may have been right in considering my venture a bold one. Subsequently he made no difficulty about admitting other sonatas; he only recommended me to be careful in their selection, and to choose those that could more easily be appreciated. I advanced therefore very cautiously, the second sonata I played being the one in D, Op. 28, commonly known as the 'Pastorale'. What a contrast 1848 offers to 1895! *Then* the question was: Can this or that sonata be understood by the audience? Nowadays the difficulty lies in finding one not too hackneyed.

These few public appearances did more for me to keep starvation from my door than the host of letters of introduction I had brought from Paris, some of them to very interesting people. One was to Lord Brougham, who received me very kindly in his mansion in Grafton Street, but candidly told me that music was not at all in his line; another was to Mr. Richard Cobden, who said with equal candour that he had never been able to distinguish 'God Save the Queen' from any other tune; a third was for Chevalier de Bunsen, the Prussian Ambassador, a most distinguished and amiable man and a great lover of music. In his family circle I have spent many a pleasant hour, although my first appearance in his 'salon' had been far from agreeable to me. I had received a very kind invitation from him to play at one of his receptions, and had set great hopes upon it, for necessarily there would be many people there who could favour my views if I succeeded in gaining their approbation. The rooms were densely crowded, everybody standing, as nearly all the seats had been removed, and a frightful babel of tongues was going on. When I was asked to play, I thought in my innocence that silence would be established and sat down to the piano; but after a few minutes I rose again with the conviction that not a note of what I had played could have been heard. The thanks of the chevalier seemed a cruel mockery; still, when later in the evening he asked me to play again, he was so amiable, that out of deference to him I did so; but unable at the moment to recollect a shorter piece than the one I had played half an hour before, I repeated it, and neither the chevalier nor anybody else detected the identity!

To another introduction, that to Mrs. Sartoris (*née* Adelaide Kemble), I owe some of the greatest pleasures I have enjoyed in London. She was indeed a rare woman, and her somewhat taciturn husband a man of vast intelligence. Both were musicians to the core, intensely enthusiastic, and of sound judgment. Their house reminded me strongly of the 'salon' of Armand Bertin in Paris, for it was the rendezvous of most of the remarkable people in London: poets, painters, musicians, all feeling equally at home, and all finding something to interest them. It is to Mrs. Sartoris that I owe my first acquaintance with Browning, Thackeray, Dickens, Leighton, Watts, Wilkie Collins, and a host of other celebrities; and it will always be my pride to have enjoyed their affectionate and intimate friendship till death removed them both. Another house, the tiniest in London perhaps, but a real gem, to which I repaired often with great pleasure, was that of Henry F. Chorley, the musical critic and contributor to the 'Athenaeum'.[1] I was always sure to find interesting men there, and met Cockburn and Coleridge, who both rose to be Lord Chief Justices of England, for the first time under his roof. He was a man of strong views, fearless in his criticism, perfectly honest, although often and unconsciously swayed by personal antipathies or sympathies. Of his oddities I shall have to speak now and then.

Slowly I laid the foundations for a new existence; pupils came to me, some of them being former pupils who had

---

[1] Chorley, a Lancastrian, was music critic of the *Athenaeum* from 1831 to 1868, and librettist for Benedict, Sullivan and others.

fled from Paris like myself and continued their lessons in London. Amongst them there was the daughter of M. Guizot, who, fallen from his high estate, was living in a modest house in Pelham Crescent, Brompton. After the sanguinary June days in Paris, during which I was tortured with anxiety for my family, I sent for them and had no rest till I saw them safe in London. Soon after a hard blow fell upon me, crushing for a time all my energies—the death of my beloved father. My grief was beyond all expression, and under the weight of memories that crowded upon me I felt as weak as a child. Stern necessity roused me at last out of my stupor; the London season was drawing to a close; a musical autumn and winter season did not then exist, and all I could hope for was to find some stray pupils and to derive from them an uncertain income.

At this crisis I received an important communication from Manchester, through a brother of my Parisian friend Leo, who was residing there. Mr. H. Leo had several times visited his brother in Paris; I had made his acquaintance and found him not only a very amiable man, but a most enthusiastic amateur of music and a great connoisseur. He held a good position in Manchester, and, as far as music was concerned, he was looked upon as an authority and deservedly so. At the end of June he came to London purposely to propose that I should take up my residence in Manchester, and he assured me, on behalf of many devoted lovers of music, that Manchester was quite ripe *to be taken in hand,* and that they thought me the fittest man to stir the dormant taste for the art. We had several interviews, and in the end, although I knew absolutely nothing of Manchester beyond that it was a large and rich town, I determined to give it a trial; on the condition, however, that a fixed number of pupils (not a small one) should be enrolled to begin work from the day of my arrival, and the further condition that I should always be allowed to spend the summer season in London, where I had been too successful already, and had made too many friends to harbour

119

the thought of abandoning it altogether.[1] Not a week had elapsed when I received the news that the pupils I had stipulated for were found and awaiting me, and I was summoned to keep my promise. Reassured as to the financial prospects of the future, and attracted powerfully by the hope of fostering the taste for music in so large a community, I proceeded to change my residence for a second time in the course of three months.

I left many friends behind, amongst whom I must name dear old Moscheles,[2] in his younger days the most brilliant of pianists, many of whose compositions, especially his studies, will remain as standard works for all time. Moscheles had often been at my house in Paris, even daily during the few months which he spent there, occupied with the composition of his second pianoforte sonata for four hands. I have indeed reason to remember that sonata, for whenever he had added twenty or twenty-four bars to the unfinished work, he came to me with the beautifully written manuscript to try them over. And in order to give them their due effect, as he said, we had always to begin from the introduction and to go through the whole sonata until the new portion was reached, so that for every twenty new bars in the finale, we played the introduction, the allegro, the andante, the scherzo, and the finale, so far as it was ready. Often I was fetched from my house even as late as midnight by the amiable and charming Madame Moscheles, because 'they had a few friends with them who were anxious to hear the sonata'. I must have played it a few hundred times in this mutilated way before, on its completion, Moscheles gave a grand evening party at Kalkbrenner's house to produce it before the artistic and

---

[1] Hallé does not mention here that he had already received an offer from Bath but, according to a letter from his wife to her sister dated September 19, 1848 (see page 147), he found 'such immense musical resources in Manchester that he could not hesitate between the two towns.'

[2] Ignaz Moscheles (1794-1870). A great pianist, at his peak, 1815-30. He settled in London in 1826 but became the first professor of the pianoforte at Leipzig in 1846 when Mendelssohn founded the Conservatoire.

literary world. It met with success, but has never eclipsed the first sonata, which remains superior to it in freshness of ideas. I am still glad that I never showed any signs of impatience during this long trial; ever since I battled as a boy with Moscheles's 'Variations sur la Marche d'Alexandre', and his G minor concerto, I had venerated his name and felt happy and proud to be chosen by and associated with him on this occasion. His good feeling towards me remained the same when I came to London, of which he gave me a proof by sending his eldest daughter to me as a pupil; at which I felt elated and which was not without a certain influence on public opinion. Benedict, Sterndale Bennett, Davison, Henry Broadwood, that prince of pianoforte makers, were amongst the other friends that I quitted unwillingly, but with the hope of seeing soon again.[1]

In Manchester I was most kindly received, especially by the German colony, which was prosperous and important. Preceding my small family by a few weeks in order better to prepare for their installation, I was introduced in a short time to most of the notabilities of the town, went through a succession of dinner parties, and, in short, was 'made much of' as the phrase goes. My pupils were ladies of the most various ages, many of them having evidently joined the ranks merely for the sake of making up the requisite number. Their accomplishments were as various as their ages, but I found goodwill and perseverance amongst all of them. One pupil gave me a great surprise. She belonged to a family considered the most musical in the neighbourhood, and brought as a test of her powers a sonata for piano and violin. When I suggested that a piece for the piano alone would be more to the purpose, she said *this* was a piece of which all at home were very fond, and she hoped I would allow her to play it for me. In answer to my ques-

Julius Benedict's opera *Lily of Killarney* is still occasionally performed, and William Sterndale Bennett's chamber music is not yet extinct. James William Davison was music critic of *The Times* from 1846 to 1879 and husband of the distinguished pianist Arabella Goddard.

121

tion if her father or a brother played the violin part, she said, 'Oh, no, I always play it alone.' Now the copy she had did not contain the violin part, and I began to feel some curiosity as to how she would deal with certain parts of the composition principally allotted to the absent instrument. The sonata was a simple one by Mozart, and the lady began to play it most correctly. Soon she came to a series of eight bars in which the absent violin had all the melody and the piano nothing but an old-fashioned accompaniment in broken chords. She played them attentively, and after four bars of this unmeaning twaddle, I heard her say to herself with deep emotion, 'Beautiful!' Shortly after she omitted about twenty bars, without apparent reason, and when I asked, 'Why don't you play this part?' she gave a never-to-be-forgotten answer, 'Oh, that is in a minor key, and papa does not like minor.' How musical must have been the family capable of expunging from every piece of music all the modulations into a minor key! I did not try to convert the papa, but the daughter had to put up with pieces in minor and soon grew fond of them.

Not long after my arrival in Manchester I had occasion to hear one of the concerts of the oldest and most important musical society of the town, called 'The Gentlemen's Concerts,' from the fact that it was originally founded in 1774, I believe, by amateurs, twenty-six in number, who constituted what may be called the orchestra, but who all and every one of them played the flute! In course of time other instruments were added, and in 1848 the modern orchestra had been completed for more than a score or two of years. The society was wealthy, would-be subscribers having generally to wait three years before room could be made for them; in consequence every artist of renown who had visited England had been engaged, and the older programmes of the concerts are remarkably rich in celebrated names. At the concert which I attended, Grisi, Mario, and Lablache sang; but the orchestra! oh, the orchestra! I was fresh from the 'Concerts du Conservatoire', from Hector Berlioz's orchestra, and I seriously thought of packing up and leaving Manchester, so that I might not have to endure a second of these wretched performances. But when I hinted at this my friends gave me to understand that I was expected to change all this— to accomplish a revolution, in fact, and begged me to have a little patience. At the next concert I was engaged to play the E flat concerto by Beethoven, and Mr. Zeugher Herrmann was invited to come over from Liverpool to conduct it, which he did with great skill, accomplishing all that could be accomplished with the unsatisfactory material he had to deal with. During the same month of August Chopin came, played, but was little understood. He remained a few days only, then went to Scotland on a visit to Miss Stirling, a pupil to whom he dedicated several of his works. The Scotch climate tried his weak constitution severely and hastened his death.

In the winter of 1848-49 I ventured upon a series of six chamber-music concerts, assisted by two modest local artists; but in spite of the efforts of my friends, who canvassed most energetically for subscribers, their total number reached only sixty-seven; the sale of single tickets for the first concert amounted to three, and to a few more for each one of the succeeding concerts. These were small beginnings indeed, but did not dishearten me. Every item in the programme was new to the small audience and received with appreciation. I felt that there was a whole musical education to make, and devoted all my energies to the task. When I began a second series in November 1849 the subscribers numbered 193, and by general desire I had to add a short series of four concerts in February and March 1850. During that winter Ernst and Piatti made their first appearance in Manchester at these concerts, and from that time remained identified with them. The summer season of '49 I spent in London, where I was engaged to play at the whole series of the concerts given by the Musical Union. My choice of pieces was then unfettered, and it was a pleasure to me to introduce many works unknown to the audience until then. Among these was Schubert's trio in E flat, the performance of which was connected with an amusing incident. Mr. Ella had written an analysis of this work, to be inserted in the programme, in which he had dismissed the 'Menuetto' with the short sentence, 'This movement is not very interesting.' When he showed me the proof on the day previous to the concert, I remonstrated and said he would probably find that this 'Menuetto' was the gem of the whole trio. He replied that he had carefully read it through, and that it had not struck him as particularly remarkable. We had a short discussion about it, but I felt I could not convince him. The conversation turned upon other things for some time, when just before taking leave he referred once more to the 'Menuetto', and said: 'Well, I do not mind making a slight change in the paragraph you object to'. He showed me the proof again, and I read to my surprise: 'This movement is . . . very interesting'. The change was indeed slight—only one word omitted—but it could hardly have been greater.

On my return to Manchester after the summer season of 1849 I found the town in a state of excitement, caused by the announcement that Jenny Lind[1] would give a concert for the benefit of the infirmary. She was then at the height of her popularity, had never sung in Manchester before, and it was natural, therefore, that every ticket should be sold long before her arrival. The hall was consequently crowded, and I was accommodated with a seat on the platform.[2] I had never heard her before and my curiosity was at the highest pitch, but the reality surpassed all my expectations. Never had I been moved by any singer as by her, and never again shall be, I feel certain. Her first air was

---

[1] The Swedish soprano Jenny Lind was twenty-nine at this date. She first sang in England, in London, in 1847.
[2] The Gentlemen's Concert Hall stood on the site occupied since 1902 by the Midland Hotel.

124

the grand scena from 'Der Freyschütz', and never shall I forget the impression it made upon me. Her singing in the first recitative of the long high note with the descent which follows, upon the words 'Welch' stille Nacht', nearly suffocated me. I was sobbing audibly, and yet this extraordinary effect was produced by the simplest means. It was indeed true art coupled with enthusiasm and unconscious inspiration. Added to this there was a perfection of execution which was itself a marvel, and I can say without fear of contradiction that we shall never hear her like again. Shortly after this concert she gave two more on her own account, which were equally crowded. Since then I have heard her often and often, and my admiration always remained unaltered. The concerts in Manchester were followed by a short tour through the provinces, during which I was engaged as pianist, and had occasion therefore not only to revel in her singing, but also to witness the enthusiasm with which she was received everywhere, and which sometimes led to great inconvenience. Crowds of people were always waiting at the door of her hotel to get a glimpse of her, and the police had often to be called for her protection. At Worcester, on one occasion, I had entered a carriage with her and the horses had drawn us about two yards when the pressure of the crowd suddenly broke both the windows, the splinters of glass flying about to our consternation. I got a nasty cut. She remained fortunately uninjured, but we had to return to the hotel, and after that I was shy of the honour of driving out with her. Whether her judgement in music kept pace with her marvellous genius as a singer I have not been able to decide, for I have seen her cry when hearing a beautiful masterpiece well sung by a good chorus, and seen her cry also when some very commonplace ditty was given by the same chorus.

At the end of the year 1849 the conductorship of the 'Gentlemen's Concerts' was offered to me, and I accepted it on the condition that the band should be dismissed and its reorganisation left entirely in my hands. This was the

125

first step towards the position which Manchester now holds in the domain of orchestral music. I had then to be satisfied, however, with attracting to Manchester a certain number of first-rate instrumentalists, mostly from London, with displacing others, changing the position of the instruments which had been absurd—the double basses, for instance, standing in front—and recruiting in the neighbourhood the best talent available. The result was a good one, much approved of by the subscribers, and from that time the cultivation of orchestral music in Manchester has been my chief delight and remains so still. That the taste for chamber music began to grow and that Ernst and Piatti were often seen and heard at my concerts I have already related. During the winter of 1849-50 I proposed to Ernst that we should give a similar concert in Liverpool. He readily assented, and, relying upon his great reputation and my rising one, we promised ourselves great success, engaged a good violoncellist, made an excellent' programme and gave the concert. The audience consisted of eleven people, four of whom were reporters! Such was the beginning of my acquaintance with that flourishing town, with the musical life of which I have since become so intimately associated.

The circle of my acquaintances in Manchester had by this time become so extended, and I had come across so many amateurs with fair voices and an ear for music, that in 1850 I was able to found the 'St. Cecilia Society', in imitation of the German 'Gesang-Verein', which dwelt in my memory from the days of my childhood. It consisted of ladies and gentlemen of the best society, at first about fifty in number, who met weekly for the study of choral works under my direction, and found such pleasure in it, and worked so well, that soon these meetings became a source of great pleasure to them and to me. The society grew from year to year, and contributed not a little to spread that intelligent love of the art which distinguished Manchester. I conducted it for many years, till my engagements became

126

too numerous, and I had reluctantly to hand it over to my friend Edward Hecht, an excellent and thoroughly reliable musician, who later on became my chorus-master, and rendered me most valuable services. Death snatched him away in the prime of life, but he is most affectionately remembered by all who knew him.

Pupils came to me in increasing numbers, many giving me extreme satisfaction by their real disposition and love for music: others there were who, like the young lady with the father who hated minor keys, offered me much food for amusement. Of these I will give only one specimen, which will stand for many.

A clergyman of middle age appeared one day at my house with the request that I should give him some lessons. He had brought a friend—a total stranger to me—in order that the friend might introduce him. This seemed odd, but did not prepare me for all the oddities that were to follow. Day and hour having been duly fixed, he came at the appointed time, armed with a music book, entered my study, and without any greeting stood before me smiling. After a few moments, seeing my astonishment, he pointed with his finger to his throat, which I took for an indication that he had lost his voice. I expressed my regret at this, when he said, 'No, no; I have only taken off the badge'. I then understood that on coming for a music lesson he had judged proper not to appear in the character of a clergyman, and had exchanged the customary white necktie for a black one. I accordingly invited him to play something in order that I might know how far he had already progressed. 'Yes, yes, immediately', he said; 'but before I do so I wish you to look at the list of my deficiencies, which I have prepared in order that you might know at once how to deal with me'. He handed me a sheet of paper, the margins of which he had ornamented with arabesques, evidently whilst musing on what he would have to write down, which paper I have carefully preserved up to the present day, and which runs as follows:—

127

LIST OF DEFICIENCIES.

1. Deficient in the shake.
2. Deficient in general execution.
3. Very deficient in the performance of scales, both diatonic and chromatic.
4. Deficient in rapidity of fingers.
5. Deficient in equality of touch.
6. Third finger very weak.
7. Extreme nervousness when playing before company.

Questions.

1. How many hours (a day) ought I to practise?
2. What style of music ought I to study?

Having pocketed this remarkable document, I renewed my request for the performance of some piece or other, and he proposed to play Beethoven's Sonata with the Funeral March, contained in the book he had brought with him. Sitting down to the piano, he looked attentively at the music and then put his fingers down upon two wrong notes—two E naturals. 'E flat', I said. He held fast to the wrong notes, looked at the music, at his fingers, up and down several times, then turned his head towards me with a smile, said, 'To be sure', and then removed his fingers from the wrong to the right notes. In the very next bar a similar mistake occurred. I corrected it; then came the same operation of looking up and down, the same smile, and the same 'To be sure'. This having been repeated four or five times in as many bars, I remained silent afterwards, thinking only of how to get rid of so unpropitious a pupil without giving him offence. He struggled on through about half the first page, which took a considerable time, then suddenly closed the book, held it before my eyes, and said, with another smile, 'Is not that nicely bound?' I assented; and 'I got it bound when I was at Cambridge,' was the information he gave me. Re-opening the book, he began again at the identical note in the middle of a bar at which he had left off, and after another ten minutes' stumbling he reached at last the end of the first page. By that time I had made up my mind, and told him politely that he was not advanced enough to become one of my pupils, and advised him to go to someone else. He was sorry, but submitted. Before leaving he said there was one piece he was most anxious to learn, and 'did I think he could master it?' 'Which piece?' I inquired; and 'A Fantasia on the Prophet, by Liszt,' was the answer; to which I could only reply: 'Not in this world!' During this last colloquy he had been putting on his gloves, which gave rise to the following little dialogue. Holding them up to my eyes, he said: 'They are very bad.' I: 'They seem to have been of service.' 'Yes,' said he. 'I am a poor clergyman, and I paid for them 3 fr. 75 c., so I must wear them a little longer.' To get away from this somewhat painful topic, I asked if he had been in France lately. 'Oh, no,' was the reply; 'I never was in France.' 'In Belgium, then?' 'Oh, no, never.' 'Well, you told me just now you had paid 3 fr. 75 c. for the gloves; where did you get them?' 'Oh, I bought them in Market Street; but,' with another good-natured smile, 'you are a Frenchman.' After which kind remark he looked at his watch and said: 'I must go quickly, I have to preach.' I resisted the temptation to follow him and hear his sermon, which in spite of his musical peculiarities may, I hope, have been a good one.

Another, this time a real pupil of mine, a gentleman of undoubted musical abilities, gave me a shock of another kind on one occasion. He played very well and was extremely fond of Chopin's music, playing many of his pieces, even some of the very difficult ones. I brought him the sad tidings of Chopin's death. 'Capital!' he exclaimed; 'now I can have his complete works bound!'

My life now became a very busy one; added to my duties at the 'Gentlemen's Concerts', many London engagements, and hosts of pupils, there came in the winter of

1855 the offer to conduct a series of operas at the Theatre Royal, Manchester A very excellent troupe had been engaged, comprising Mme. Rudersdorff, Mme. Caradori, Mlle. Agnes Büry, Herr Reichardt, Carl Formes, and other remarkable vocalists. Most of the operas were given in German, and it was happiness to me to conduct really first rate performances of 'Fidelio', 'Don Giovanni', 'Der Freyschütz', 'Die Entführung aus dem Serail', alternately with more modern works such as 'Robert le Diable', 'Les Huguenots', 'La Favorita', and others. Madame Rudersdorff was one of the most dramatic and accomplished singers I have ever listened to, and achieved a real triumph as Leonora in 'Fidelio'. Formes was at the zenith of his powers and equally admirable as Leporello or as Don Giovanni. Reichardt was a charming tenor who sang Belmonte in 'Die Entführung' to perfection, and all were musicians to the core, having their heart in their work.

The public appreciated our efforts, but nevertheless the pecuniary success of the season was not complete, the expenses being too great, and daily performances during several months being more than a town like Manchester could digest. The obstinacy of the *entrepreneur* and proprietor of the theatre, John Knowles, who never listened to a counsel however well-meant or useful, was also a drawback. His peculiarities were many and sometimes amusing; thus, when Formes, then one of the foremost singers in any country, sang the part of Don Giovanni and insisted upon having a bottle of real champagne in the finale, we could never bring Knowles to consent to give it; he would rather have dispensed with the performance altogether. The consequence was that on such evenings I came to the theatre with a bottle under my cloak, and was probably called a fool for my pains by the excellent Knowles. On one occasion 'Lucrezia Borgia' was to be performed, the numerous minor parts in which were distributed amongst the best of the chorus singers. Coming to the last rehearsal on the morning of the performance I was met by the stage-manager, who told me with a long face that, by order of Mr. Knowles, the doors of the theatre would be closed that evening, and no 'Lucrezia Borgia' performed. On my inquiring for the reason of this totally unexpected step he answered, 'All the *nobles* want half-a-crown apiece.' The nobles meant the minor parts, and there were about eight of them. I satisfied them out of my own purse and the performance took place, much to the satisfaction of Mr. Knowles, who, however, never alluded to my interference. During this same performance a perplexing accident occurred, nearly causing a break-down. Formes at the last rehearsal had earnestly asked me to make a cut of eight bars in one of his airs, to which I had assented. The cut was duly marked in all the orchestral parts and observed in the evening; but, lo! Formes had forgotten all about it, made no cut, and sang the eight bars to which there was no accompaniment. To jump back with a whole band was an impossibility; all its members were however immediately aware that something was wrong and had their eyes upon me. For a moment I wondered what was to be done; but soon there occurred a chord upon which I seized, made the band hold it out pianissimo and allowed Formes to sing to it what remained of the eight bars, as a kind of cadenza, until he had rejoined us, when we jogged on together again. The best of the joke was that he was not aware of the trick he had played us, or that there had been anything unusual; such a thing would, however, not be possible with any but Italian music of the Bellini and Donizetti school.

From the year 1850 I had commenced to give pianoforte recitals, until then unknown in England. In London I gave them for several years at my own house, until I transferred them to St. James's Hall. In other towns I chose the most suitable concert-rooms, and found willing ears nearly everywhere. The programmes comprised every kind of pianoforte music, and if at first I avoided the more abstruse works, such as the later sonatas of Beethoven, I soon discarded this precaution and played whatever I wished to make known. Beethoven, Mozart, Haydn, Bach, Weber, Hummel, Dussek, Scarlatti, Rameau, Mendelssohn, Schubert, Schumann, Chopin, Heller, and others were put under contribution, and all the pleasure which the evenings at the Guiberts' house in Paris had given me was renewed on a larger and more public scale. Of the towns besides London and Manchester which I have thus visited and visit still, there is none to which I have gone more constantly and with more pleasure than Edinburgh, or where I have found a more intelligent and music-loving public. Friendships formed there have still further endeared the town to me, and amongst these friends stands out conspicuously Georg Lichtenstein, who, after being aide-de-camp to Kossuth, was exiled from Austria, and after months of trouble had settled down in Edinburgh as music-master. He is no more, and I am therefore at liberty to say that it would be difficult to find a more accomplished, versatile, genial, and, above all, upright and kind-hearted man than he was. His conversation, always full of charm, and touching often upon the political events in Hungary at the time of the insurrection, in which he had been an actor, has made many an hour delightful and memorable to me. To his kindness in correcting the proofs of my local programmes I owe it that they were free from blunders, which was often not the case in other towns, where I had not an opportunity of revising them myself. Thus on one occasion when I had sent a programme to Scarborough, which included a 'Caprice brillant sur la Truite (Schubert), by Heller,' I found it printed to my horror as 'Caprice brillant sur *La Trinité*'!

In the winter 1852-53 the number of subscribers to my 'Chamber-Music Concerts' in Manchester had largely increased. I therefore constituted them into a 'Chamber-Music Society', with an influential committee, keeping the entire management in my own hands. The room in the old town hall, very favourable for music of the kind, was not

132

very large, holding about 450 seats.[1] These were all
subscribed for, and there was a list of from 80 to 100
would-be subscribers who had to wait for vacancies. Such
gigantic strides had the love of music made in three years.
The visits of Ernst, Molique, Sainton, Vieuxtemps,
became now regular, and Piatti was the violoncellist at all
the concerts.[2] The intimacy with these men, great artists
all, forms one of my happiest recollections. They were
always guests in my own house, and we revelled in music.
Good old Molique with his broken English, the meaning of
which had often to be guessed at, was a subject of constant,
harmless amusement. As we were taking a drive together
one day, Molique, thinking the driver had lost his way,
leaned out of the cab and shouted: 'Coachman, *who* are
we?' translating the German 'wo' (where) by 'who'. He got
the immediate reply: 'Well, sir, if you don't know who you
are I cannot tell you.'

Molique had a horror of cats, but, strange to say, our cat
was attracted by his playing and was generally found
sitting before the door of his room when he practised,
which greatly disturbed him when he opened it, and could
not muster courage to pass out or to drive it away. Piatti,
who occupied an adjoining room, never failed before re-
tiring to bed to catch the cat and hide it under Molique's
bed. When Molique discovered the intruder a most
ludicrous chase began, lasting sometimes an hour and
more, as he did not dare to approach the cat, but tried to
drive it away by merely hissing at it.

Molique was a great executant, knowing absolutely no
difficulties, finding easy what gave trouble to all other

[1] The old town hall was in King Street, Manchester. It was superseded by Waterhouse's
famous building in 1877 and later demolished.
[2] Bernhard Molique (1802-69) settled in England in 1849 after twenty-three years as
leader of the royal orchestra at Stuttgart. Prosper Sainton (1813-90) was another
violinist who settled in England in 1845 after a distinguished European career; he
became professor at the Royal Academy of Music and leader of the Covent Garden
orchestra, under Costa, for many years. Henri Vieuxtemps (1820-81) was among the
greatest violinists of his day, and his concertos are still played; one of his brothers was a
cellist in Hallé's orchestra for many years.

133

violinists; but his style was polished and cold, and he never carried his public away with him. Ernst was all passion and fire, regulated by his reverence for, and clear understanding of, the masterpieces he had to interpret. Sainton was extremely elegant and finished in his phrasing, but vastly inferior to the others I have named. Vieuxtemps, whose appearances were more rare, was an admirable violinist and a great musician, whose compositions deserve a much higher place than it is the fashion now to accord them. Of Piatti, the incomparable, I need not say a word beyond this, that during an intimate friendship, extending over forty-six years, my admiration of the artist and my love of the man have gone on constantly increasing. He is the only one remaining to us of the above-named quintet; the others are now listening to the harmony of the spheres.

The Chamber-Music Society was dissolved in 1858, when the institution of my orchestral concerts no longer left me time to devote the attention to it which it imperatively required. The five years from 1852 to '57 were uneventful; the summer seasons were spent in London with my family, which had rapidly increased, the autumns and winters in Manchester, leaving time, however, for my peregrinations to provincial towns, both in England and Scotland. During my annual sojourns in London I made the acquaintance of Robert Browning and his gifted wife, who were both passionate lovers of music, and especially of Beethoven's sonatas, which I had often the privilege of playing to them at my own house in Mansfield Street. Browning formed an exception to the rule that poets and literary men care less for music than painters, in whom the love of our art seems almost invariably to be inborn. Thackeray and Dickens had a certain liking for music, but Tennyson listened to it with great indifference, and his loud talk whilst I was playing some superlatively fine work has now and then 'agacé' my nerves. Browning knew the whole literature of music, had an unfailing judgment, and sometimes drew my attention to pieces by older masters which had escaped my notice and which I have always found worth knowing. He must have been a good pianist himself, but I could never prevail upon him to give me a proof of his powers as such. I enjoyed his friendship to the end of his days, and he endeared himself to me especially through the kindness with which he forgave my incapacity to understand his poetry—an incapacity which I frankly confessed to him more than once.

Meyerbeer I had the pleasure of meeting again in London, admiring, as before in Paris, his high-bred manners, his cultured *esprit,* invariable tact, and great *savoir-faire.* One day my friend Chorley had a small dinner party, composed of the then Lady Hastings, two other ladies, Meyerbeer, Costa, and myself. The conversation fell on Mozart's 'Zauberflöte', which had been given at Covent Garden a few days before. Lady Hastings had not enjoyed the performance and abused the work in unmeasured terms. Especially was she angry with the recitatives; 'those interminable, monotonous, unmeaning recitatives,' she called them. Meyerbeer looked puzzled, Mozart's opera containing no recitatives, and asked quietly: 'Quels sont donc les récitatifs dont Lady Hastings parle?' 'Ils sont de moi, monsieur,' said Costa, and Lady Hastings began to talk of something else.

Spohr also visited London during one of the seasons I spent there, and I was happy to be able to speak with him once more of my childhood, and to express my gratitude for the kindness he had shown to me when I was a boy. He attended one of the concerts of the Musical Union at which I played one of his pianoforte trios and also a sonata by Beethoven, the one in D major, Op. 10, No. 3. After the concert he came into the artists' room, said some flattering things to me about my performance of the latter, and added, 'a fine sonata'; then, with a tone of astonishment, 'und gar nicht veraltet' (not antiquated); a remark with which I totally agreed, but which struck me as very superfluous.

135

In 1856 Manchester began to prepare for the 'Art Treasures Exhibition', which was to be held in the following year, the musical part of which was entrusted to me. The committee—Sir Thomas Fairbairn (then Mr. Fairbairn) was chairman— acted with unparalleled energy, and succeeded in bringing together a marvellous collection of masterpieces of the different arts, such as I believe has never been equalled since. Her Majesty the Queen visited the exhibition, and how successful its whole career was, what hosts of distinguished visitors it drew to Manchester until its close, is too well known to dilate upon here. I was most anxious that music should hold its own, and not suffer by comparison with the other arts. To this end a first-rate orchestra was absolutely necessary, an orchestra better than the one of the 'Gentlemen's Concerts', which, though a vast improvement upon what it had been before, left still much to desire. Fortunately the committee agreed with my views, placed ample means at my disposal, and I succeeded, not without considerable trouble, in bringing together a thoroughly satisfactory band by engaging competent performers from London, Paris, Germany, Holland, Belgium, and Italy, in addition to the best of our local players. Concerts took place every afternoon, but I conducted only on Thursdays. They were much enjoyed by crowds of visitors, and soon became one of the chief attractions of the exhibition. Thousands and thousands of people from the northern counties there heard a symphony for the first time, and it was interesting to watch how the appreciation of such works grew keener and keener almost with every week. The whole exhibition was like a beautiful dream, justifying its motto, 'A thing of beauty is a joy for ever!' and its elevating and refining influence cannot be over-estimated. As usual, the catalogue had its humorous points by accidental interchanges of numbers: thus a picture of King Lear on his death-bed was described as 'There is life in the old dog yet,' and you could daily hear the remark 'How true!' when passing it. Another,

Charles Hallé in the 1850s

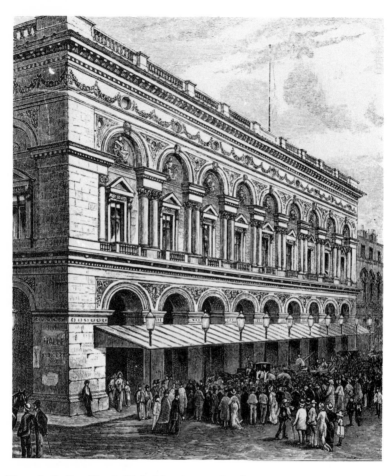

The rebuilt Free Trade Hall, Manchester, shortly
after its opening in 1856

Charles Hallé aged 70

Season 1895. 96
First Violins

	£	s.	d.
Brodsky	5	.	.
Jacoby	1	10	.
Akeroyd (Misc.)	1	1	.
Bauerkeller	1	1	.
Bridge (Misc.)	1	1	.
Briggs	1	1	.
Campione	1	1	.
Gaggs (Misc.)	1	1	.
Harndorff	1	1	.
Hatton	1	1	.
Heiss	1	1	.
Hunnemann	1	1	.
Kettenus	1	1	.
Klippe	1	1	.
Nidub	1	1	.
Dow (Misc.)	1	1	.
	21	4	

Hallé's last entry in his account book, written a few days before his death representing a madman sitting stark naked on the bare ground with his arms clenched round his knees, was called 'Portrait of Lord John Russell.' An old man was heard to remark, 'Probably when he was out of office!'

To this exhibition I owe my intimate friendship with Richard Doyle—Dicky Doyle, as he was called familiarly—the genial, gifted humorist and delightful companion. My acquaintance with him had been slight, but sufficient to warrant my inviting him to be our guest for a few days, and so to see the exhibition. He came, promised to stay three days, and remained two months, to our intense delight. Daily we studied the marvellous pictures together, and he opened my eyes to many beauties which I might have passed by. He was no less quick in seizing upon any comical figure that presented itself in the motley crowd, and many were the pen-and-ink drawings which in remembrance of them he put on paper during our quiet evenings at home, and which I preserve carefully. An oddity in the railway arrangements during that time I cannot leave unnoticed: a single ticket from London to Manchester cost then 33s., but a return ticket (from London to Manchester and back) cost only 21s., and several times have I seen people, who in ignorance had taken single tickets, exchange them, when enlightened, for return tickets, and receive 12s. into the bargain. The ways of railway directors are mysterious sometimes.

When the exhibition closed its doors in October, 1857, the orchestra which I had taken so much trouble to form, and which had given such satisfaction, was on the point of being dispersed to the four points of the compass, never to be heard again in Manchester. This was excessively painful to me, and to prevent it I determined to give weekly concerts during the autumn and winter season at my own risk and peril, and to engage the whole band, trusting to the now awakened taste for music for success and perhaps remuneration. The necessary preparations retarded the execution of this project until January 30, 1858, when the first concert took place before a scanty audience.[1] I was not disheartened, for I remembered how the Chamber Music Society had grown from small beginnings, and judged rightly that the crowds who had thronged the exhibition did not specially come for the music, and that concerts offering nothing but music, and at necessarily higher prices of admission, stood upon another footing. I felt that the whole musical education of the public had to be undertaken, and to the dismay of my friends I resolved to give thirty concerts, and either to win over a public or to fail ignominiously. The 'Gentlemen's Concerts' were an exclusive society; none but subscribers were admitted and no tickets sold. Before my advent they had never even published the programmes of their concerts, and the directors had only done so since 1850 at my earnest request, because I objected to conducting concerts of this clandestine sort. To the public at large symphonies and overtures were therefore *terra incognita,* and it was not to be expected that they would flock to them at once.

Beethoven's symphony in C major headed the first programme and was vehemently applauded by the meagre audience. The loss upon the concert was a heavy one, and was followed by similar losses week after week, until my friends were debating whether for the sake of my family I ought not to be locked up, and I myself began to feel rather uneasy. It was not before nearly half the series of thirty concerts had been given that things took another aspect; the audience gradually became more numerous and more appreciative; at last full houses succeeded each other, and the day after the thirtieth concert my managers and dear friends, Messrs. Forsyth Brothers, brought me, with the statement of receipts and expenses, ten brand-new threepenny bits, the profits on the whole series—a penny per concert! Perfectly satisfied with this result, which I considered most encouraging, I at once made

[1] A Saturday night and it was raining!

138

arrangements for a second series to be given during the winter season 1858-59. It consisted of twenty-seven concerts, but for the third series I reduced the number to twenty, and opened a subscription list, which soon was adequately filled, showing that high-class orchestral music had taken hold of the public and that my ventures of the previous years had borne fruit. Since then those concerts have continued to prosper and have now reached their thirty-eighth season. The orchestra, at first only sixty strong, has gradually been increased, until for the last ten years it has numbered upwards of one hundred performers, and added to it is a chorus of three hundred singers of uncommon excellence, for the performance of oratorios and secular choral works. It is not my intention to write a history of these concerts, I shall only allude now and then to some of their more salient features, such as the production of new or neglected works; but I can look with a certain pride at the catalogue of works performed up to the present time (summer 1895), which comprises 32 oratorios, 71 other choral works, 110 symphonies, 214 overtures, 205 miscellaneous orchestral pieces, 183 concertos with orchestral accompaniments, and minor pieces without number. In 1860-61 the concerts had to suffer an interruption, as I was called upon to conduct a season of English opera (organised by Mr. E. T. Smith) at Her Majesty's Theatre in London, which counted Mmes. Sherrington and Parepa, Messrs. Sims Reeves and Santley, among its artists.

The most remarkable feature of the season was the production of two new English operas, the 'Amber Witch', by Wallace, and 'Robin Hood', by Macfarren, neither of which however took hold of the public in spite of some very clever and some charming pieces admirably sung. Both operas are forgotten now. Other works such as the 'Bohemian Girl', 'Fra Diavolo', in English dress, and 'La Reine Topaze', by Massé, also given in English, were more successful and drew larger audiences. All were sung and

139

acted to perfection. One performance of the first-named of these operas I remember still with considerable amusement on account of an odd incident. It had been substituted for another work in which Mr. Sims Reeves had the principal part, this gentleman having sent word in the morning that he was suffering from hoarseness. When in the evening I was crossing the stage to go to the conductor's desk the call-boy ran after me shouting, 'Mr. Hallé, we have forgotten the child!' This very child has to be seen sitting at the window when the curtain goes up, and in ten minutes I had to commence the overture. 'Go, fetch one quick,' was my answer. 'All right,' said he, disappeared, and before three minutes had elapsed he came back with a struggling girl, about five years old, in his arms, and followed by an apple-woman whose daughter he had unceremoniously captured in the Haymarket. The child was carried off to be dressed whilst the mother was pacified by the stage manager, and I was able to begin the overture at the appointed time. At its conclusion I rang up the curtain with some diffidence, but there sat the child, neatly dressed, at the window with the nurse, and we proceeded quietly with the opera. In the first scene where the Polish Count (Santley) takes leave of his daughter before his departure from home, the little girl is brought to him and he has to sing a touching and rather lengthy farewell ballad. So the child came down on to the stage, but the moment she saw the foot-lights and the public behind she yelled with fright, screaming at the top of her voice. Santley, however, was equal to the occasion. He knelt down, threw his large cloak round the girl, took her head under his arm and kept it in chancery, all the time singing his ballad with the utmost pathos, unmindful of the kicking feet and struggles going on under the cloak, hardly perceived by the public. Madame Parepa, a most excellent vocalist with a splendid powerful voice, was of a colossal size, which led to an amusing scene on the occasion of the performance of 'Fra Diavolo', in which she took the part of

140

Zerlina. When in the bedroom scene Zerlina undresses and remains clad in white, Madame Parepa looked simply enormous. Standing before the looking-glass, admiring herself, she has in the English version the unfortunate words to say:—

> There really is not much amiss
> When you can boast of a figure such as this.

The moment she had uttered them the whole house roared with laughter, renewed again and again. After the performance Mme. Parepa asked me innocently if I knew what had happened to make people laugh so much, being totally unconscious that she was herself the cause of the hilarity.

Another unrehearsed effect enlivened one of the performances of 'Robin Hood'. Mme. Sherrington was Maid Marian, and Mr. Sims Reeves Robin Hood. In the last scene Maid Marian brings the reprieve to Robin Hood, condemned to death, and waving it rushes at him from the farthest end of the stage. On this occasion Mme. Sherrington came down with such impetuosity upon Mr. Sims Reeves that he, unprepared for the onslaught, was toppled over, his head coming close to the footlights, and Maid Marian on his back. Unable to shake her off at once, he raised his head and blew with all his might into the footlights which were nearly singeing him, thereby causing an hilarity amongst the audience sufficient to play havoc with the concluding scene of the opera.

The season being brought to a close, I returned to Manchester with the intention of producing during the following winter some interesting and striking novelty at my concerts. After a good deal of cogitation I fixed upon some of Gluck's operas, banished from the stage, for which therefore the concert room would be the proper place. 'Iphigénie en Tauride' was the one I chose first,[1] remem-

---

[1] Hallé's chronology is wrong here. He had produced Gluck's *Iphigenia in Tauris* before the London opera season.

bering how the dramatic power of the music had in my younger days in Paris drawn tears from my eyes when I was simply perusing the score. From this self-same score I had to copy the whole of the orchestral parts, none being printed, and Gluck's scores being so carelessly engraved, with so many and such extraordinary abbreviations that to confide the task to an ordinary copyist was out of the question. Chorley undertook the translation of the libretto, Messrs. Chappell published a neat vocal score, and on January 25, 1860, the work was performed in the Free Trade Hall, Manchester, with an enormous success. Mme. Catharine Hayes, Messrs. Sims Reeves, L. Thomas, and Santley, were the interpreters, and could not well be surpassed in their respective *rôles*. It had to be repeated several times during the season, and Messrs. Chappell undertook a similar performance in London under my direction, and with the same artists, which was equally well received. This led to another private performance, remarkable in many ways. Lord Dudley, that munificent patron of the arts, asked me if I could give the work in his own noble gallery, with a small orchestra and chorus, and on my answering in the affirmative he left me *carte blanche*, stipulating only that the very best vocalists should be engaged, namely, Mme. Titiens, Messrs. Sims Reeves, Belletti, and Santley, and that the band should include Messrs. Sainton, Piatti, Lazarus, and others equally well known. I set to work at once, trained a small but efficient chorus from the Italian Opera, and after a few rehearsals one of the most exquisite performances that I have ever been privileged to listen to, took place. To my surprise Lord Dudley had invited but few friends, about forty, to share his pleasure; but he was thoroughly satisfied; said to me repeatedly that he had never had so fine a concert in his house, and requested me to call the next morning with the bill of costs. When I drew this up the sum total was so enormous that I felt some anxiety as to how it would be received, fearing that his satisfaction of the previous day might be somewhat damped. I handed it to him, and whilst examining it he spoke again of the pleasure the performance had given him, made a few pencil strokes on the document, wrote a cheque and handed it to me, saying, '*I have doubled all the terms;* it is the only way in which I can show my entire satisfaction.' Such princely generosity is rare indeed, and I was amazed; still more so when he added, 'Can you arrange for a second performance soon? But (with a smile) I suppose it will not be necessary to double the terms again.' The second performance did take place about a fortnight later and gave equal satisfaction to all concerned.

Having produced 'Iphigenia' for the first time in England, I turned my attention to another of Gluck's masterpieces, 'Armida', the translation of which had in the mean time been completed by Chorley. The printed full score of this opera, dating from 1778, is, if possible, in a worse and more misleading state than that of 'Iphigenia'. I could not, therefore, confide the task of copying out the orchestral parts to an ordinary copyist. Anxious, however, to be spared such a labour myself a second time, I applied to Berlioz, whose knowledge of Gluck and all his works was complete, Gluck being one of his idols, and asked him if the parts of 'Armida' could be obtained in Paris, where this opera had been so often given in former times. I received the following reply, interesting in more than one sense:—

My dear Hallé[1]—I congratulate *us* on the brilliant success of your attempt to reveal Gluck to the English. So it is true that sooner or later the flame bursts forth, however thick may be the layers of rubbish under which one thought it smothered. This success is prodigious, when one remembers how little the 'Iphigénie' can be appreciated at a concert, and how closely Gluck's works in general are bound up with the stage. All the friends of what is eternally beautiful owe you and Chorley a great debt of gratitude.

There are no other separate parts of 'Armida' except those

[1] Translation.

of the Paris Opera, and they certainly would not be lent to you. Moreover, they contain a host of arrangements formerly added by Gardel and others, and additional instruments inserted by I know not whom, of which you would certainly not make use. Your intention is to produce Gluck *as he is*. You will, therefore, be forced to have the parts copied from the score, which, however, is one of the least faulty and the least untidy which Gluck has left us. For some unknown reason the composer nowhere employs the trombones in it; it is the same in 'Iphigénie en Aulide'. In 'Orphée', 'Alceste', and 'Iphigénie en Tauride' on the contrary, this instrument plays a very important part. In 'Iphigénie en Aulide' Gluck has made some *changes* for certain passages, and written some *dance-music* which is only to be found in the MS. score belonging to the Opera. You cannot make your English edition very exact without coming to Paris. But if it is only a pianoforte edition the harm would be less great. I think there never existed a lazier composer than Gluck, nor one more careless of his works, of which, however, he seems to have been very proud. They are all in the most complete disorder and disarray.

I have not, to my knowledge, been attacked by Wagner; he merely replied to my article in the *Débats* by a pretended explanatory letter which no one could understand. It was an inflated and bombastic letter that did him more harm than good. I did not answer a single word. Farewell, my dear Hallé, pray remember me to Madame Hallé, and say a thousand kind things to Chorley when you see him.

H. Berlioz

The musical phrase which Berlioz quotes at the end of his letter occurs in Iphigenia's grand air in the second act, 'O malheureuse Iphigénie', and, with its melodious, wonderfully vast sweep, is one of those inspirations which even a great genius finds but seldom, and thoroughly deserves the notes of admiration added by Berlioz.

I had now to give up the hope of getting the coveted parts from anywhere, for they had never been printed, so I sat down and wrote them out myself, as I have done for 'Iphigenia'. Trying as the labour was it was still one of love, and I felt fully recompensed when on September 28, 1860, I conducted a performance which unfolded hitherto unknown beauties to a vast audience. The success of 'Armida', if somewhat inferior to that of 'Iphigenia', was still great enough to reward me for my trouble. Many years later I had the additional satisfaction of being able to lend my parts to Mme. Jenny Lind Goldschmidt for a performance at the 'Rhenish Musical Festival', only made possible by the happy circumstance that I had them in my possession.

Letters

[Translated from the German]

London: April 27, 1848

My dear Parents—Forgive me for not having written for so long; courage failed me to do so; I could not make up my mind to give only bad news, and of good news, alas! I had none to give. The Revolution has dealt me an incalculable blow, from the effects of which I shall have to suffer for a long time. Paris is in a sad and pitiable state, and God knows if it will ever recover itself; that my position there, at least for the present, is quite lost, you will already have guessed. All my colleagues are in the same case. I have been here in London three weeks, striving hard to make a new position, and I hope I shall succeed; pupils I already

145

have, although as yet they are not many. The competition is very keen, for, besides the native musicians, there are at present here—Thalberg, Chopin, Kalkbrenner, Pixis, Osborne, Prudent, Pillet, and a lot of other pianists besides myself who have all, through necessity, been driven to England, and we shall probably end by devouring one another. During the last few days I have begun to hope, as I have several times played in public with great success, and trust soon to have got my footing. Until now, sadness has been the order of the day, but, I assure you, my courage does not fail me. My family has, of course, remained in Paris, and you can easily fancy that, all alone, I do not feel very happy.

O damnable Revolution!

Should things mend in Paris, I shall return there after the London season; but should they remain in the same condition I must of necessity establish myself here and bring my family over, for in Paris one might starve—there will be no thought of music there. In Germany, also, everything seems in hateful disorder—madness is at home everywhere . . .

Carl Hallé

[From H. Leo]

Manchester: August 4, 1848

My dear Mr. Hallé—According to your wish, I hasten to inform you of the state of things here, so that you may come to a decision on your return. . . . My opinion has not changed in the very least, and should you resolve upon coming to Manchester, it is my innermost conviction that your success will be complete. . . .

You will feel the delicacy of my position with respect to you. I should so heartily rejoice to have you here, and yet, believe me, I would not let myself be so swayed by selfishness as to give you advice against my own convictions. Were you my brother, I should say: Come to Manchester. All the same I cannot and must not, accept the responsibility of the step. If you feel the courage and strength to trust Manchester with your fate, I believe you would do right, and would not regret it, but if you will not take the risk we must submit, and only beg you to give us credit for our good intentions. The post is closing; perhaps I shall write a few lines to-morrow if anything occurs to me.—Ever yours.

H. Leo

[From Hallé's first wife Désirée to her sister in New Orleans; translated from the French]

3 Addison Terrace, Victoria Park,
Manchester: September 19, 1848

. . . . Meanwhile let me tell you that we have been at Manchester since the 6th of this month; Mathilde's last letter informed you that Charles, having received proposals from this town more advantageous than those from Bath, had decided to establish himself here, where, moreover, he finds such immense musical resources that he could not hesitate between the two towns. He has hardly been here a month, and we may already hope to see him occupy a magnificent position; half his time is taken up with lessons, and on all sides he is being asked to give a series of musical matinées like those he gave in Paris; Mr. Leo, who induced him to establish himself here, and who is our good angel, told me last night that they would bring him in at least eight thousand francs a year; last Wednesday he played a Concerto of Beethoven's for the Amateur Society; he obtained a magnificent success; I never saw such great and general enthusiasm; during the concert he was offered an engagement to play at the forthcoming Liverpool Festival; his name is so well known throughout England that a London publisher came to Manchester yesterday to offer to take all his compositions, at the rate of ten francs the printed page. . . .

If you could only see all Charles's goodness to us; his heart inspires him with charming deceits; thus he had written to me to London that Manchester not being a city of pleasure, he had not been able to find a furnished house, and had been obliged to take the only house that had been offered to him, and that it was a very ugly one, which annoyed him greatly, for our life here having to be entirely a home-life, he would have wished at least to give us the pleasure of being well-lodged. Judge of our delight, the evening of our arrival, to find a charming little

147

house surrounded by delicious gardens, situated in the middle of a park, and with all the comforts of an English habitation, carpets everywhere, &c., &c. His pupils and good Mrs. Leo, in order to welcome us, had lighted up all the rooms, in which were placed large baskets of flowers; you should have seen poor Charles's joy, how he rejoiced like a child at our glad surprise... It would be impossible, dear sister, to tell you the immense happiness that filled me at that moment, which would alone sufficed to make me forget the past six months. . .

The inhabitants of this town are very kind; they seem so proud of possessing an artist like Charles, that they try to guess what would give us pleasure; all the best society hastened to call upon us; we are overwhelmed with invitations and visits. We have found a real father in Mr. Leo, it would be impossible to be more devoted than he and his wife are to us; they managed to spare me all the annoyance of furnishing by persuading one of their friends, who was going to Germany, to let us, for 12l. a month, the delightful little house we occupy. Life is much cheaper than in Paris.

[To H. F. Chorley; translated from the French]

Manchester: August 23, 1850, Greenheys

My dear Chorley—I hope you are aware that, before leaving London, I made several attempts to find you at home, but they were all in vain, to my very great regret; for I wanted greatly to have a long talk with you; and to ask your advice once more as to the change of residence that I have so long projected, without having yet been able to put it into execution.

One good conversation is worth more than a lengthy correspondence, but nevertheless, if you will have the goodness to answer a few words to the questions I shall put to you, I shall always greatly profit by them, and shall be very grateful, believe me.

The idea of establishing myself in London has so ripened in my mind that I begin to think that I shall carry it out this winter; it seems to me, at least, that I could never find a more favourable moment; the death of Madame Dulcken,[1] and Benedict's

[1] Louise Dulcken (1811-50), pianist and sister of Ferdinand David, settled in London in 1828 and was a popular figure in the musical scene.

departure, must leave a momentary void which may, perhaps, make a prompt success more easy. If I still hesitate a little, it is solely because my position here is really a very good one, and the thought of losing it, without soon finding at least an equivalent one, torments me on account of my family, which is a large one, as you know. You will understand therefore, my dear Chorley, why I ask my true friends, and I count you among them, to aid me by their counsels and to indicate, as far as may be, the means that might serve to render success more prompt and more easy. I know too little of the *terrain* of London to be able to ask you precise questions, excepting this one however: At what time of the year should you advise me to arrive? would it be necessary for me to come before the month of January or February? As to all the rest, I trust in your good nature; I know that you will give me all the advice you can, and I promise to follow it with gratitude.

If you can enter into details, even as to the part of the town that you would recommend me to reside in, do so, I beg of you; you will forgive my indiscretion, I hope, in virtue of the importance of the question.

Another thing I would ask you, my dear Chorley, is that if you have any doubts as to my success in London, you will tell me so as a friend, and without circumlocution, and to place you more in a position to do so, I will tell you frankly, between ourselves, that I earn between 1,200l. and 1,300l. a year here; this will explain my hesitation.

I repeat, my dear Chorley, that all your advice will be received with gratitude, and let me hope that you will bear me no ill-will for giving you so much trouble.

A thousand affectionate compliments from my wife and from your sincerely devoted friend,

Charles Hallé

[To Mr. Renshaw, Director of the Manchester Concert Hall; translated from the French]

Manchester: August 14, 1851, Greenheys
My dear Renshaw—I think, with you, that the pieces Beale

proposes are as old as the hills, but what can we do? There is a trio in 'The Magic Flute' ('Dunque il mio ben non vedrò più?') which you might suggest, but I do not think there is one in 'Le Prophète', rather in 'Les Huguenots'; but it is especially against the duets that we must rebel, we have had them four hundred times, at least, and there must be others in existence, perhaps there are some in the 'Prophète' and certainly in 'Robert' or 'Les Huguenots'. I know no more of Mlle. Fischer than you do, but I think that for a concert at which Madame Sontag is to sing we rather need a male singer than another lady, and for this reason I should prefer Stigelli; whom have we besides?

The air of Stradella, the one from 'Saffo', and the Spanish songs will be interesting; Tamberlick ought to sing something else besides the eternal 'Tesoro';[1] 'Piff, paff' would only do with orchestral accompaniment, which we were unable to procure last time, when Formes wanted to sing it. Tamberlick sings the air from 'Fidelio' very well, provided that it prove effective in a concert room; propose it to him, anyhow.

As to the overtures, I think that for the first concert those of 'Preciosa', 'Fra Diavolo' and 'Nozze di Figaro' will suffice; next Wednesday we shall try some new ones for the second. For the rest I perfectly approve of your programme, and if you will come to the rehearsal on Wednesday we can talk of it further.

A thousand kind regards from your very devoted

Charles Hallé

Extracts from a diary, 1855-56

Translated from the German

December 12, 1855

Rehearsal at the Concert Hall in the evening. Haydn's B Major Symphony, Overture, *Ossian*, Gade, the second movement of Berlioz's Symphony, 'Harold in Italy' ('Marche des Pélerins'), and a triumphal march by Best, for next week's concert.

---

[1] He sang it, nevertheless!

Tolerably satisfied with the orchestra, but still further convinced of the necessity of the intended reforms. Gade's overture is pretty and shows good intentions, but is wanting in strength and in breadth of idea. In the present dearth, however, its appearance must be accepted with thankfulness. Berlioz's movement carried me back to the dear old days, and therefore, perhaps, gave me exceptional pleasure. But how fresh, even at the present day, is the old master's, Haydn's, Symphony!

December 18, 1855

The necessity of engaging a trumpet-player for to-morrow evening's concert took me to the theatre, where a pantomime rehearsal was going on. Knowles, in his usual abrupt manner, spoke to me of a plan which certainly deserves consideration. He proposed that I should ask the committee of the New Free Trade Hall if, and on what terms, they would let it to me for a year, or for a shorter or longer period, and that he and I should make use of it together.

December 19, 1855

Molique arrived towards four o'clock and accompanied me in the evening to the Concert Hall. His presence fired the violinists, and altogether the performance was not unsatisfactory. The effect of the whole was marred by the laughable figure and manners of the singer, which were not redeemed by any artistic qualities. A clarinet concerto in A by Mozart was capitally played by our excellent clarinettist, Grosse. The composition, although by Mozart, is such a grandfatherly production and so lengthy that the finale had to be left out, not to try the patience of the public beyond endurance. Mr. Best[1] had come from Liverpool to hear his march, and introduced himself to me after the concert, but it was impossible to find anything agreeable to say about his composition.

December 20, 1855

To-day's concert, the third, was not quite so well attended. The approach of Christmas, the cold weather, and Jullien, who is performing his hocus-pocus for the first time at the theatre, were

[1] For many years organist of St George's Hall, Liverpool, and the Handel Festivals.

151

perhaps the reasons that militated against it. The programme was as follows: Quartet, C major, Mozart; sonata with violin, C minor, Beethoven; pianoforte quartet, F minor, Mendelssohn; violin duet, G minor, Spohr; Barcarolle, Frühlingsglaube and Erlking, Schubert and Liszt. Molique was very well disposed and played splendidly. The duet was played by him and his pupil Carrodus in a masterly fashion. The concert was quite satisfactory, with the exception of the viola player, who caused us great anxiety. I was tolerably content with myself, but have often played better.

December 21, 1855

Molique and Tolbecque left for London this morning at 9 o'clock; Lucas remained till 5. During the day I busied myself with the buying of Christmas presents, and in the evening the Christmas-tree arrived; it is a stately one.

December 22, 1855

The preparations for Christmas continue. The children are very busy on their side, and the whole house is full of secrets. M. is not quite well, but I hope she will be all right by Monday evening, so that we may be able to enjoy the feast in the old accustomed manner.

December 23, 1855

Dined with Mr. Henry Higgins. After dinner, with him and Mr. Renshaw, we held an improvised meeting, under Higgins's presidency, upon the affairs of the Concert Hall, and brought them into order. My proposal and stipulation was that, instead of the irregular and approximate fortnightly rehearsals of two hours' duration, there should in future be *one* rehearsal the day before the concert, and of longer duration. The concerts must therefore be changed to Thursday, and dates fixed longer beforehand. Everything was willingly granted, whereupon I withdrew my resignation.

Very busy in the evening decorating the Christmas-tree.

December 24, 1855

The dear, familiar Christmas Eve made us all, great and small, very happy. The gifts to the children were rich, and their delight

152

filled our hearts with joy. The children had again prepared a small tree for us in their school-room, and pleased us, moreover, with little gifts of needlework, drawings, and dear letters. Until 10 o'clock they revelled in their happiness, which was to begin anew the next morning. I received a nice present from Mr. Stern, the 'Conversation's Lexicon', in twenty-three volumes, and Mendelssohn's 'Lieder ohne Worte', beautifully bound, from an anonymous but well-known hand. I gave my wife a neat gold bracelet and necklace, which greatly pleased her.

December 25, 1855

On this Christmas Day the children made closer acquaintance with their new treasures, and I, during the time, went over some new music. Gade's 'Spring Fantasia', a very thoughtful and pleasing work. Schumann's 'Paradise and the Peri' truly surprised and entranced me; of all his works not one has so deeply interested me; it has great poetic charm; melody and harmony are new and very fine. It is a pity that the poem is somewhat monotonous, and must probably diminish the effect of the music, because it requires too many slow *tempi*. Began Marschner's 'Vampire'.

December 26, 1855

Practised Molique's trio diligently, and continued Marschner's 'Vampire'. At the Concert Hall rehearsal in the evening I announced the renewal of my engagement to the members of the band, which was received with jubilation; further, the changes in the regulations concerning the performances and rehearsals, which also met with approval. Afterwards, with the quartet alone, went through Berlioz's symphony, 'Harold in Italy', and brought the first three movements to a satisfactory point. After the rehearsal I went to the first performance of the pantomime, 'St. George and the Dragon', the unbounded stupidity of which annoyed me; public taste in England is still rather backward. The performance of 'Elijah' at the Concert Hall is fixed for January 22, and Banks's concert at Ashton-under-Lyne postponed to the 23rd.

December 27, 1855

Spent a few hours of the day very pleasantly; Canon Toole (a

Catholic priest), a very nice, enlightened, poetry and art-loving man, brought the children a big magic-lantern, and many interesting pictures were thrown upon a white sheet fastened to the wall. Before Canon Toole left us, a remark about Shelley led to a theological discussion between him and Miss C. What a sharp contrast—an unbeliever and a Catholic priest!

December 28, 1855

Finished reading Marschner's 'Vampire'. The work contains many beauties, and exceeds in true worth many of Meyerbeer's operas which enjoy such a far greater celebrity. It is to be regretted that so many of the incidents seem copied from the 'Freischütz'.

Piatti writes that his wife is better, and he hopes to be able to come on Wednesday. Received a letter from Chester; they do not want a Beethoven Sonata for their concert on January 2, but something lighter.

December 29, 1855

An article in the 'Manchester Guardian', under the title, 'Mr. Hallé and the Concert Hall', speaks of the new regulations which I made known to the orchestra. The directors most likely will not approve of this publicity, but it is necessary and useful for the whole institution. The 'Guardian' also draws attention to Molique's trio.

Began to write the score of Méhul's G minor Symphony. The work seems fresh and interesting.

For some time past I have read a great part of Schlosser's 'Welt-Geschichte', and have much enjoyed the solid worth of the work; the craving after knowledge and learning has strongly revived in me; I thirst for a quiet time when I can better satisfy my longing for reading.

December 31, 1855

The last day of the year; a day on which there was little work to do, I spent it quietly and cosily in the midst of my family. Made music, and read a good deal. In the evening delighted the children very much by making them some weak punch before they went to bed, and making them drink the health of their grandmamma, their parents, and their aunts. The few hours before midnight I spent in alternately reading Schlosser and conversing with my wife, and so peacefully and quietly ended the year.

January 1, 1856

At midnight peacefully and contentedly greeted the New Year with a glass of punch. The children were all quietly wrapped in slumbers free from care; we parents went the rounds to give them each a first loving New Year's kiss. The past year has brought us many joys and much good, and has had few shadows: may the coming one be as favourable. Seldom has the looking back been so pleasant, and though there have been many cares, they are none of them discouraging.

January 2, 1856

Started for Chester at 8.45, and went to the Royal Hotel. At 11 looked up Mr. Gunton to talk over the performance of the 'Messiah', which must take place without a rehearsal. Mr. Gunton is organist at Chester, and in the absence of an orchestra had undertaken to accompany the 'Messiah' on the organ. Upon my natural inquiry as to whether the chorus was safe, I received the surprising answer that he had never heard them; so that conductor, chorus, solo-singers and organist for a great performance met for the first time in the hall, and at the moment of commencing the concert! Nevertheless everything went well; the chorus was excellent (from Liverpool), the organist also, the solo-singers, Madame Rudersdorff, Miss Messent, Miss Dolby, Mr. Lockey, and Mr. Thomas altogether left very little to be desired, and so the conducting was not unpleasant. A young bass-singer Cuzner, made his *début* in the air 'Why do the Nations', and gave proof of a good voice. After the morning concert wandered through the quaint old town, and visited the famous cathedral, where the carved wood-work of the choir is specially remarkable. In the streets the arcades over the foot-ways struck me most. At the evening concert I played Lizst's 'Lucia', Caprice in E by Mendelssohn, 'La Truite' by Heller (as an encore, impromptu by Chopin); two 'Lieder ohne Worte' by Mendelssohn, and a waltz by Chopin.

155

January 3, 1856

Left Chester at 9.10 and reached home at half-past 11, where I found Molique and Piatti waiting for me; both had arrived the previous evening. The concert was very gratifying, and gave me personally great enjoyment. Programme.—Trio, Beethoven, Op. 70, No. 2; sonata with violoncello in A, Op. 69, Beethoven; trio in F, Op. 52, Molique; Souvenir d'Ems, Romanza, and 'Les Fiancés', petit caprice for 'cello, Piatti; Serenade, Op. 56, Heller, and Mazurkas in B, F minor, and C, Chopin. Beethoven's two magnificent works were played as perhaps we had never played them before; Molique's new trio is highly interesting, and made a deep impression. Molique was recalled, and the dear good man was as much moved by the affection with which we had played his work as by its reception by the public. For me it will always remain a pleasant recollection that I have, so to speak, brought this trio to light. Piatti's little solos were, as usual, played in masterly style. I, too, was satisfied with my playing, in spite of a little slip of memory in Heller's Serenade. Both friends left for London at 4 a.m. Piatti was anxious about his wife, and Molique went to bear him company. I sought my bed at 1 o'clock, very tired.

January 4, 1856

The 'Guardian' and the 'Examiner' have very laudatory articles on the concert, especially on Molique's trio, so that the apprehended danger that unfamiliarity with the work might cause dissatisfaction with it, and thus affect its reception in London, is happily averted. Set my library in order, and sent a quantity of books and music to Anderson, the bookbinder. In the evening continued to write the score of Méhul's symphony, and busied myself choosing the works for the next concert.

Put the last touch to the corrections of the first twelve sonatas by Beethoven for the new edition.

January 5, 1856

To-day's 'Athenaeum' attacks Jenny Lind pretty severely for her rendering of the solos in the 'Messiah'; Chorley's personal likes and dislikes seem to have an influence upon his pen, without his will or knowledge. Wrote some more of Méhul's symphony; the first movement is half finished; the ideas are fresh and noble; but the workmanship and power are not very interesting, but somewhat trivial.

January 6, 1856

Ella writes that he wishes to give some lectures on music in Manchester; he seems to have already entered into the matter with Mr. Andrews, who referred him to me. I have promised to use my influence, and have asked for more particulars. Busy with a mass of correspondence that had got into arrears. Mr. Banks, who came to inquire about the programme for his coming concert, told me he had heard Jenny Lind in the 'Messiah' at Liverpool; according to him she has fallen off, and the applause, though still great, was not to be compared with the enthusiasm of former days.

January 7, 1856

For the next concert I have chosen the sonata by Beethoven. Op. 27, No. 2, never yet played by me in public, and am working hard at it. Spohr's trio in F will also be given, and require some preparation.

Have finished the fourth volume of Schlosser's 'Welt-Geschichte', thus terminating the history of the old world, which was rich in enjoyment.

January 8, 1856

Have finished the sketch of the programme for four private concerts to be given during the winter months, and have sent it to Mr. Higgins for perusal; it contains much that is new and interesting, and I shall be pleased if it is accepted, although I have prepared much hard work for myself by it. Ella writes that he has already given up the intention of giving musical lectures in Manchester. He has not yet decided to give concerts before Easter, and maintains that everything in London is at a standstill, except Jenny Lind, who seems to monopolise the public.

Have written to Molique to consult him as to the best construction for the new platform that is to be erected in the Free Trade Hall.

January 9, 1856

Began the Andante of Méhul's symphony, which seems to be very simple.

157

Busied myself with the analysis of Spohr's trio in F, and the Beethoven sonata.

Began to read about the Arabs in Schlosser.

January 10, 1856

Chappell, the publisher, has at last consented to allow my new edition of Beethoven's sonatas[1] to proceed in chronological order, instead of in the arbitrary order, or rather disorder, of Moscheles' edition. I have commended him much for it. The analysis of Spohr's trio for the next programme is finished and sent to the printer.

January 11, 1856

Have half finished a long letter to my mother, which will give her great pleasure, as it contains a full description of our Christmas doings. The children had an invitation to Professor Scott's,[2] but were kept at home by the cold weather, so after dinner I consoled them by playing with them for a whole hour—building palaces, lighthouses, and such like with their little wooden bricks. In the evening I worked at the symphony, and practised. A duet for piano and violin upon 'William Tell', by Osborne and de Bériot, which I shall have to play next week with Mr. Cooper, vividly reminded me of a *soirée* at Madame Huët's fifteen years ago, when I played it with Alard.

The thought of going once again to Paris and playing at the Conservatoire has greatly occupied my mind to-night.

January 12, 1856

Auguste Gathy writes from Paris asking for biographical notes for an article on me in his 'Musical Lexicon'. He congratulates me upon the situation I have won in England.

In the evening worked hard at Méhul's Andante, so as to be rid of it, as my interest in the work begins to diminish.

January 15, 1856

Left for Wakefield at 12.40. Before starting I bought a good edition of the 'Vicar of Wakefield', and by its perusal changed an otherwise tedious day into a very pleasant one. The place

---

[1] Still in print until 1964, when all remaining stock was destroyed by fire.

[2] Professor A. J. Scott was first Principal of Owen's College, the forerunner of Manchester University. He collected much material for a Chopin biography.

itself is most prosaic, dark, and smoky, as are all English manufacturing towns, and in no way answers nowadays to Goldsmith's description. I arrived at 4 o'clock and went to the Strafford Arms—a very old-fashioned building, with old-fashioned management and service. I met there Mr. Perring and Mr. Wynn, who take part, like me, in to-night's concert. They are both indifferent singers, but possessed of a certain amount of instruction, and very much in earnest. The givers of the concert—Mr. Cooper and Miss Milner—only want talent to make them very good artists. The concert took place at 8 o'clock at the Exchange Rooms—a large hall with good acoustic, and before a large audience. My share of the programme consisted of Osborne and de Bériot's duet, the Finale of Lucia, by Liszt, Caprice in E major, by Mendelssohn, and Heller's Truite (as an encore, 'Lied ohne Worte' in A, by Mendelssohn), variations from Beethoven's Kreutzer Sonata, and an impromptu and two waltzes by Chopin. The appreciation of the public, among whom was the former celebrated singer, Miss Wood, was flattering. The first duet, however, did not go well at all. After the concert I took a stroll through the principal streets of Wakefield, and returned to the hotel, where I had a tolerably long conversation with Mr. Perring.

January 16, 1856

Finished the 'Vicar of Wakefield' in bed this morning, and therefore rose late. At 12.30 started for Leeds in company with Mr. Perring and Mr. Wynn. The programme was identical with that of last evening. I had even greater success than the day before, and after Chopin's Waltz had to play two Mazurkas (in B and C Major). An Erard piano was sent to both places for me. During the day I went to an exhibition of French paintings, and was specially struck by the powerful conception and vigorous execution of Rosa Bonheur's picture of the Horse Fair. The grouping of the spirited, snorting horses is wonderful, and there reigns a mighty lifelikeness in the whole work. Very remarkable is the new, nearly completed, town hall—a building that does honour to the town of Leeds, and that will have few rivals in England.

Bought a fine-bound Virgil (in Latin) with the date of 1548, also an English translation of Juvenal and Persius.

January 17, 1856

Left Leeds at 7.20 and arrived at Greenheys towards 10 o'clock. Piatti and Sainton arrived at 3 o'clock, and we began the rehearsal for to-night's concert at once. Programme: Trio in F, Op. 123, Spohr; Sonata quasi Fantasia, Op. 27, No. 2, Beethoven; trio in B, Op. 97, Beethoven; Variations *à la Monférine,* piano and violoncello, Hummel; *Morceau de Salon,* violin in D, Sainton. The trio in B gave us special pleasure, and made a great impression on the public, as also did the Sonata, which I played with a little hesitation. During the concert we were pleasantly surprised by a little supper of oysters and champagne, arranged by some friends. Heron, the Town Clerk, presided at it. Piatti and Sainton left again at 4 a.m. After the concert we entertained ourselves for a time with the game of cannonade.

January 18, 1856

Very busy the whole day, so that I felt the fatigue of the previous day's exertions doubly. Dinner at Mrs. Grundy's where I met Professor Scott and his wife, with the poet C. Swain, and spent a very interesting evening. Some little pieces I played to them were gratefully welcomed.

January 19, 1856

In the few free moments my pupils left me I practised hard the duet for piano and viola on themes from 'The Huguenots', by Thalberg and de Bériot, as I have to play it next week at the concert with Mr. Blagrove. Very unpleasing and uncongenial work, which I have to force myself to. In the evening choral rehearsal at the Concert Hall for the 'Elijah' which takes place next Tuesday. In precision of intonation the chorus leaves much to be desired, but I have tried to give them an idea of the importance of *nuances,* and in this I have partly succeeded. At any rate, they have become more attentive. But, so long as the chorus does not have regular practice, good results cannot be expected. To this end, let us hope, the new Free Trade Hall will soon contribute.

January 20, 1856

A letter from Molique, with a very good plan for the building of

160

the orchestra in the Free Trade Hall. I am entirely satisfied with it, and hope to get it adopted. Sainton writes he can accept an engagement at the Concert Hall for February 21. I offered an engagement, through Molique, for the same date, to Miss Leusden, recommended to me by Hiller. She seems to be a very good contralto. Mr. and Mrs. Troost and Mr. Kyllmann visited us in the morning. The latter criticised the too rapid speed of the *tempo* of the Finale of the Beethoven Sonata at the last concert, and he may have been right.

At 3 o'clock I dined with the Charles Souchays, and spent a most agreeable afternoon. A noble and intellectual family, such as one rarely finds. During dinner, among other things, much talk of the pleasantness of the life in many parts of Germany, and the beauties of my birthplace, which they knew by report, were sung by me. Later, I played some short, delicious pieces of Heller's, which led to some very interesting conversation. A letter from Mendelssohn was read, in which he expresses the opinion that words are vague, and capable of many interpretations, whilst music renders feelings with precision. Against this there is very much to say. Altogether, the letter seems to me more ingenious than true. The Heine was much talked of, and I had many anecdotes to tell of our former close acquaintanceship in Paris. When the conversation turned upon painting, Mrs. Souchay asserted an opinion, against which I protested, that a painter can only reproduce the impression of what he has actually observed in nature. For instance, he could only paint the sorrow on a human countenance that he had really seen there.

January 21, 1856

Worked again at that fatal Thalberg duet, and looked more closely through the three Schumann trios, in order to choose one for the next concert. The third seems to be the best.

In the evening choral and orchestral rehearsal of 'Elijah'. Of the solo singers only Miss Birch put in an appearance. The chorus did better, and the orchestra was really good, and so the performance promises to be satisfactory.

January 22, 1856

Went to Mr. Blagrove in the morning to arrange for a rehearsal

161

for this afternoon, and then to Mr. Peacock to lay the plan for the orchestra before him, which met with his entire approval. We went together to the new building, which is pretty well advanced, and I was much surprised by the size and beauty of the different rooms. But it seems to me that in the great hall the space allowed for the orchestra is too small, and especially is it to be feared that the desire of gain, or, at any rate, of material profit, will not be brought into accord with the necessary arrangements for real artistic purposes.

The performance of the 'Elijah' this evening was in many respects satisfactory, though the soloists left something to be desired. According to old-established custom, the public gave no sign of approval throughout, which naturally was not encouraging to the performers.

January 23, 1856

The concerts that have lately taken place in the surrounding towns have given me the notion of attempting a so-called *tournée* myself, and I have already written to Sainton and Piatti about terms.

At 6 in the evening started with Miss Poole, Miss Manning, Miss Wilkinson (a young pupil of Garcia's), Mr. Blagrove, Mr. Frank Bodda, and Banks in an omnibus from the Mosley Arms Hotel for Ashton-under-Lyne for a concert. This was largely attended by a somewhat raw and unintelligent public; the reaction upon me was such as to make me very dissatisfied with my playing, and altogether I could not work myself up to concert pitch. We returned in the same omnibus, and I reached home very tired at midnight, and with the fear that the Broadwood piano I had sent there might be injured by the dampness of the hall.

January 24, 1856

The programme of to-day's concert in Bury was the exact counterpart of last night's. The public quite as numerous, but very intelligent and appreciative. I have seldom played better; my pieces the same as last evening: Beethoven's Sonata in C. Op. 53, Thalberg and de Bériot, Heller's Truite, and the Finale of Lucia by Liszt. The duet pleased so well that part of it had to be repeated, and after Liszt's Fantasia I had to play Mendels-

sohn's 'Volks-' and 'Frühlingslied' as an encore. The whole
evening, as well as the drive there and back, was very pleasant,
and reconciled me to the whole undertaking.

January 25, 1856
Sainton writes that he usually gets 30 guineas a week during a
tournée, and leaves it to me to decide what I shall give him; this
would be very acceptable, but the project cannot be realised
before the coming season as it requires too much preparation,
for which I cannot spare the time. We shall see later on. Piatti
sent an undecided answer.

Third concert to-night; at Cheetham, in the new Town Hall.
Very empty room. The programme the same as last night and
the night before.

January 26, 1856
Studied the second Schumann trio (F major) and Heller's
'Wanderstunden' and 'Nuits Blanches' for the next concert, and
the last-named filled me with the intensest pleasure. Later went
through some of Bach's Motets, which are to be tried next
Monday at the St. Cecilia.

January 27, 1856
Worked at the analysis of Schumann's trio for the next concert,
in which I proffered the opinion that the German element
contained in Schumann's works, and which has some affinity
with the spirit of Jean Paul, militates somewhat against a right
understanding of them in other countries.[1] Worked at the trio
itself, as also on the little Heller things. Some of Schumann's
'Noveletten' I played through with delight.

January 28, 1856
Finished the analyses of the trio, and also of Beethoven's A
minor Sonata, Op. 23, and took them both myself to Sever,[2] who

[1] Hallé also suggested that over-estimation of Schumann's works in Germany ten years
earlier had created a counter-reaction in England. 'We hope, however,' he wrote, 'that
the time will come when the English public, sufficiently familiarised with Schumann's
works, will recognise their real merit and accord to him that distinguished place in the
history of music which he is entitled to hold, for although he can never be ranked with
the greatest masters, yet no one . . . will deny him the quality of a true poet-
musician.'
[2] Cave and Sever were Manchester printers.

was greatly pleased with the first. Ordered at Mr. Hulme's a large mirror for our drawing-room as a surprise for my wife.

The St. Cecilia was not well attended, most likely on account of the cold and bad weather; the Bach Motets caused great interest, and promised us many pleasant hours. They will be studied with affectionate industry. After the meeting went with Mr. Hecht, Dr. Finckler, and Mr. Wydler to the Clarence, where we chatted agreeably for an hour or two. On the way back I asked Dr. Finckler to give me some lessons in Latin, and so fulfil a long-cherished wish, and we fixed next Friday evening for the first lesson.

January 29, 1856

Worked diligently for the next concert. The trio by Schumann pleases me more and more. Also the Noveletten become clearer and dearer to me; the ear becomes accustomed to some rather considerable harshness. An Étude by Kullak, 'Les Arpèges', I played through, which promises to be a brilliant and pleasing drawing-room piece. Went through some parts of Bach's Mass with astonishment and admiration. In the evening wrote a few pages of the score of Mozart's 9th Concerto in G major.

5

Postscript: 1865–95

By C. E. Hallé

With letters and diary extracts, 1858–90

I⊤ has been left to me to record the last thirty years of my dear father's life, to take up the pen which dropped from his hand the day before he died, and to conclude the task he left uncompleted.

It will be a labour of love to recall and chronicle those events in his life at which I either personally assisted, or of which he spoke to me in the intimacy of our friendship—a friendship which never from my earliest childhood to the day of his death suffered the slightest break, or was marred by even the most transient misunderstanding . . .

It will be in vain for me to attempt to make this chapter as interesting and amusing as those that have gone before. Apart from my very inadequate power as a chronicler, my father repeatedly told me that what he would have had to say about the last thirty years, the period from 1865 to 1895, which has been left to me to record, would be sadly lacking in interest after the story of his youth and the most exciting portion of his career.

In undertaking the task I suffer from the extreme disadvantage of not being a musician myself when so much of

¹ Slightly abridged from *Life and Letters*. Omitted passages are indicated by three dots.

what I have to say is connected with that beautiful art, of which my father was such an ardent disciple. A great love for it I do indeed possess; my childish ears were made familiar with the noblest creations of Beethoven, Schubert, and Bach before I left my cradle, and as my childhood and boyhood—owing to delicate health—were spent at home, music was the daily accompaniment of my life. In short I have never ceased to feel that my early familiarity with all that was most beautiful in the art of music developed an understanding in me for other forms of beauty which otherwise I might never have possessed. And thus my own experience has made me rightly understand the importance of the work my father accomplished during the many years he laboured to bring music to the ears and hearts, not only of the rich, but of the most humble. . .

It is impossible to believe that some element of refinement has not been developed in the large audiences of working men who, standing and packed together in great discomfort as I have often seen them, have yet listened for hours, and evidently with much appreciation, to most intricate and delicate music; or that the taste thus formed in one direction should not have had its effect in others, and possibly have coloured their whole lives.

Every evidence of such appreciation was very dear to my father, and the three following letters, treasured among his papers, were found after his death, along with many others of the same kind. The first, from an anonymous correspondent, must have been written in 1864:—

How slight and subtle may be, and ofttimes are, the links of that electric chain whose vibrations arouse in our hearts memories and thoughts that have long lain buried there! These and similar thoughts filled my mind at the sight of a programme—a programme of the eighteenth concert of the seventh season of Charles Hallé's unrivalled orchestra. Seven years ago he led such an orchestra, and drew from the keys of his pianoforte such harmonies and melodies as beforetime were reserved exclusively for the wealthy. In the glass building prepared for the exhibition of Art Treasures we first listened to him, and the strains of that delicious music floating through the building became so associated with all that is most beautiful in painting and sculpture, that it is almost impossible to separate them. And when the first notes of his band peal through the Free Trade Hall, that noble, but now somewhat dingy, room becomes transformed into a fairy palace, bathed in summer sunshine, and instead of a closely packed and (except in the reserved seats) plainly-dressed audience, we see groups of gaily-attired ladies, or distinguished-looking men sauntering through the galleries of paintings or gazing on the glittering armour, or students intently absorbed in the contemplation of some remarkable work of long ago. But we will suppose the day a Thursday, the time 2 P.M., and by one accord the loungers are drawing towards the orchestra; the discordant sounds emitted from various instruments being tortured into tune subside; a slight, fair-haired man bows slightly around, takes his place, raises his bâton, and the first note of some lively overture, or it may be of some enchanting symphony, floats through the nave, enchanting the listener, who perforce almost holds his breath, lest he should lose one note of that sweet music; while over all glows the brilliant sunshine, and the scent of summer air floats through the building. Under such circumstances we first heard Charles Hallé, and often as we have attended his concerts, the charm has never failed. Last night—a wet, splashy February evening—every sense of discomfort was dispelled, and all our interest absorbed in the music, as if we heard it for the first time. A very few moments after the time named on the programme Charles Hallé appeared, and the hush of pleased expectation stole over the miscellaneous company assembled at the Free Trade Hall. Glancing over the orchestra, we recognise many familiar faces—Seymour in his accustomed place, though the lapse of years has left unmistakable signs on his face and figure, still discourses sweet music on his violin, which he handles as if he loved it; now he plays seriously, not as in bygone times, when one has seen his gravity disturbed by the frolicsome Jacoby; the latter has now subsided into a grave middle-aged man. De Jong is still there—and Baetens—but Richardson is gone, and some few others we miss. From this reverie we are aroused by the sharp tap of the bâton, and a flood of music flows around. This dies away—a vocalist has the next part—then again the instruments have their turn; all is delicious, but we wait for the treat of the evening, Charles Hallé's solo on the piano; the silence which had previously reigned deepens and becomes intense as we watch his fingers fly over the keys, wooing the music from them. If it did not seem fanciful, I should say the sensation is almost that of playing on one's very heart-strings—we almost forbear to breathe. To those who have not heard him I cannot convey any idea of the power and sweet-ness of Hallé's playing; while those who have had that pleasure need no words on the subject from me. . .

The next letter was written on a long narrow sheet of paper such as is found in workshops:—

Nov. 10, 1873

Dear Sir,—Having had the pleasure of attending your first concert this season, I beg to tender you my best wishes for your future success; and not having had the pleasure of hearing such a display of talent before, I felt most delighted, and beg you will please accept the small token I forward you.

Respectfully yours,

An Operative

The small token consisted of two yards of fine white flannel, which my father carefully preserved for many years.

The following is the second of two letters, the first of which has been lost, from an old member of his Manchester Choir:—

King City, Missouri, U.S.A.
November 16, 1884

Dear Sir,—Your kind letter of October 16, enclosing your photograph, came duly to hand, for which please accept my heartfelt thanks.

On looking at your photograph, your features seem so

lifelike that you don't seem to have altered since I last saw you, which is over twenty-two years ago. May you long live and look as well!

I enclose you a copy of my photo., taken the day I was sixty years old. I do not know if you will be able to recognise me. I still keep up my interest in choral music. I conduct a small society here, and play the organ at church, and teach the Sunday-school children to sing. This I have to do in what little time I can spare from business. I have given it up several times, thinking I was getting too old, but no one seemed to take it up; and I hated to see the young folks without any one to lead them. So went at it again. I guess I shall have to die in harness yet; but the proverb says, 'It is better to wear bright than rust.' Hoping we may meet where harmony never ceases,

I remain, dear sir,

Yours very truly,

WM. DICKENS, Senr.

Dealer in lumber, coal, and farm machinery.

My father had always the greatest respect for his audiences, of whatever sort they might be, and never gave them anything but the very best at his command, whether it was his own playing or the performance of his orchestra. My mother used to relate how on one occasion, soon after his arrival in England, he and Ernst the violinist, with whom he was touring in the provinces, arrived at a small town where amateurs of music were so few that scarce a dozen persons had assembled to hear them. From the artists' room they could see how small was the audience, and simultaneously exclaimed: 'Then we must play as we have never played before!' They kept their word, and at the close of the concert the impulsive, highly-strung Ernst threw himself into my father's arms, saying, 'Hallé, we never played like that in all our lives!'

To bring his band by training and careful recruitment as near perfection as possible was the hobby of his life, and to this end he spared neither trouble nor expense. He never for a moment allowed any question of money to stand in his way, and his agents were often driven to despair by his engagements at ruinous terms of artists who did not make the difference of a sixpence in the receipts; indeed, to my certain knowledge, he several times gave cheques to members of the band, or to singers whom he engaged for the concerts, on his private banking account, so that he might escape the 'talking to' he knew he so well deserved, if Messrs. Forsyth had got wind of his goings on.

It is not for me to say anything about the excellence of the Manchester orchestra, or of the chorus which he also formed there. They have been heard in London, and the orchestra has played in all the leading provincial towns in England, and at Edinburgh, Glasgow, Dublin, and Belfast, so that they are both well known. . .

To give a list of all the works for orchestra and the piano which he introduced for the first time in England would include a large proportion of all the choral works, symphonies, concertos, and chamber music ever produced here; nor was this all he achieved in the cause of music. He edited a complete set of Beethoven's sonatas, besides executing endless other editorial works, and compiled a School for the use of Students of the Pianoforte, which by easy grades should conduct them from the elementary to the most difficult stages of the art. He was largely instrumental in founding the Royal Manchester College of Music, which had been the dream of his life ever since 1852, when he elaborated his scheme in a correspondence, now unfortunately lost, with Mr. Adolf Meyer, but which was only fulfilled in 1893. He was elected first Principal of the college, and took the liveliest interest in his duties and in the progress of the students, but he was snatched away after two brief years of labour in this field, in which he had hoped to accomplish so much.[1]

My father's industry was perfectly astounding, and he

---

[1] He was succeeded as Principal by Adolph Brodsky, whom he had invited to be principal violin professor at the College and leader of his orchestra.

170

must have had a constitution of iron, in spite of his delicate health as a child, to go through the amount of fatigue he did without apparent discomfort. He was incessantly travelling; but railway journeys, however long, never seemed to tire him. Many and many a time he would travel, say from Manchester to Edinburgh, conduct a rehearsal in the afternoon and a concert in the evening, and return to Manchester the same night, reaching home at four or five o'clock in the morning, and yet after a few hours' sleep he would be quite fresh again and ready for his next day's work. Many and various were his adventures on these journeyings, and he was never tired of relating them. On one occasion he was snowed-up in a train in Scotland, and he and his two or three fellow-travellers were nearly starved, when the guard remembered that a fine pig had been placed in the van. This unfortunate animal was promptly converted into pork chops over the engine fire and furnished an excellent supper, in spite of his shrill protests at being immolated for the public good. Another time the train he was in broke down, and as he was to play at a concert that evening he was sent on to his destination in a tender attached to the engine. He dressed for the concert as he went along, and the two good-natured stokers helped him into his clothes; but their valeting left marks on his shirt-front, which caused much amusement among his audience when he at last reached the concert-room.

Another most amusing adventure was also connected with the break-down of a train. On this occasion my father had a band of some fifty members of his orchestra with him, and after a long and tedious delay it occurred to one of them to express his feelings of strong dissatisfaction at things in general by an improvised solo on his instrument, which happened to be a bassoon. This encouraged others in different parts of the train to join their lamentations to his, each man on his own instrument, and soon night was made hideous by the most lamentable sounds ever suggested by the goddess of despair. Presently there came a

171

move on the part of the train of a few yards, when flutes and clarinets set up the liveliest airs of rejoicing; but again there was a stop, and fresh wails of anguish smote the astonished air.

My father was mightily enjoying the *charivari*, and Mr. Straus, who was with him, was preparing his fiddle to take part in it, when, happening to look out of the window, they discovered they were not in the open country as they had imagined, but in the suburbs of a town. The inhabitants, awakened out of their virtuous slumbers by the appalling din, were leaning out of doors and windows in night attire, with flat candlesticks in their hands, evidently by their gestures protesting against the performance of the Hallé band, but the noise was so great they could not be heard. Fortunately at this juncture a fresh engine arrived, and the train escaped wreckage at the hands of a population goaded to fury.

'I little thought I should ever travel with a life-boat on either side of the railway carriage,' he once quietly remarked on his return from a concert in the Midlands at the time of a great flood. On our inquiring if he had got wet, 'No,' he said, 'the water did come in a little, but I put my feet up on the seat, and fortunately the engine fire was not put out.' No difficulties or hindrances ever prevented him from doing all that was humanly possible to keep his engagements. . .

Railway journeys, even unattended by adventure, always gave him a certain amount of pleasure; he liked them, he liked the rapid movement of the train, the certainty of a few hours' respite from his incessant occupations, and, strangest taste of all, he adored Bradshaw. Nothing pleased him better, if any of us were going a journey, than to look out the trains, and the mention of an expedition to the Continent took him away from any other occupation to arrange the whole tour, and present us with a way-bill with the time of departure and arrival of all the trains we should take neatly written out in his beautiful handwriting for our guidance.

The only thing he thoroughly disliked was when the trains did not keep their time. I well remember the first occasion on which he went to Rome, the country was in flood, as Italy usually is in autumn, and the bridges broken, which is also not an uncommon occurrence, and we were taken round by Ancona instead of taking the usual route. Of course my father worked it all out in Bradshaw, and timed our arrival accordingly; but, alas! for the calculations of that trusty book, twelve hours after we were due in the eternal city we were still slowly crawling through a romantic but desolate-looking region somewhere in the centre of Italy, where the only food obtainable was bad coffee, green apples, and unripe grapes; and it was then my father gave vent to his sentiments—he did not say much, it was only 'What would I not give to be in a railway carriage on its way from London to Manchester,' but it summed up his opinion of Italy and all things Italian better than torrents of abuse. It was not till we had been a day or two in Rome under the excellent care of those admirable caterers to the wants of their fellow-creatures—the brothers Genre, of the Hôtel d'Angleterre—that he forgot the impression of that most lamentable journey.

My father was a most delightful travelling companion; his interest in everything was intense. He enjoyed his holidays immensely, and the most trivial incidents afforded him a fund of amusement—his great love for beautiful scenery and keen appreciation of painting and architecture made it a real pleasure to go with him where such things were to be seen. I well remember my first expedition abroad with him; it was to Hagen, his native town, when I was about fifteen, and this journey was a very momentous one for me, as after I had duly made the acquaintance of all my German uncles, aunts, and cousins, I was taken to Düsseldorff, and afterwards to Paris, and given the choice of the two schools of painting. I elected to remain in Paris, and was put under the care of my dear kind old friend, M.

173

Victor Mottez, and worked in his studio for a year. Mottez was a pupil and great friend of the famous Ingres, so that during the happy months I spent with him I made the acquaintance not only of that great painter but of many others of my father's early friends in Paris, more especially Stephen Heller and Hector Berlioz, whom I used to meet almost every Sunday evening at the house of Madame Damcké, and who always spoke of my father with the greatest affection; *le Bayard sans peur et sans reproche* was Berlioz's description of him. . . I always look back with keen interest on the time I spent in Paris, as I gained an insight into the artist life my father describes so graphically in the early pages of his memoirs and letters. He evidently intended to say a great deal more about the many interesting people he knew in the twelve years he spent in Paris (between 1836 and 1848), as his MS. shows that he broke off in the middle of an anecdote about one of them, Spontini, to go on with his own tale, evidently intending to go back to that part of his memoirs and greatly augment it.

It must, indeed, have been a wonderful society in which my father spent his time during those years. He has dwelt more especially on the musicians with whom he had inter-course; but in the long conversations I had with Stephen Heller in 1886, when I painted his portrait, many and many a name occurred of men famous in literature and art who were their daily associates. Victor Hugo, Balzac, Alexandre Dumas and his son, Alfred de Musset, and Scribe, were but a few of the brilliant host who daily met and dined, or took their coffee together on the Boulevards. I asked Heller one day when he was talking of those times and the days he and my father spent together, which of all these men had left the most vivid impression on his mind; without a moment's hesitation he answered, 'Alfred de Musset'. He told me that it did not matter who was present, nor who was talking—Hugo, Balzac, Heine, or Dumas—everybody ceased when Alfred de Musset opened his lips—his individuality and personal fascina-

174

tion were so great. There has never been in the world's history, I suppose, a time when so many remarkable men in literature, music, and art lived together as were found in Paris during the twenty years from 1830 to 1850, and where are they all now? Only two are left that I know of, our dear old friend Manuel Garcia,[1] who is still with us here in London, and bears his ninety years without a sign of discomfort, and my old master, Victor Mottez, who lives in retirement at Bièvres, near Paris. These two have still memories which are green, and many a tale have I heard from them of the sayings and doings of these many merry men of genius; for merry they were, in spite of the struggles and poverty in which so many of them lived. This aspect of their lives was forcibly brought home to me by my father a few years ago. I was going out to dinner, and noticing that my waistcoat was showing marks of age, I went to my father's study to conceal the ravages of time by the application of a little ink to certain white patches which do not usually form portion of an English gentleman's evening dress. My father watched my operations with the keenest interest and delight, and when I asked him what he saw in my threadbare garment to cause him so much happiness, he told me that what he saw reminded him of his early days in Paris, when an ink-bottle was the one essential requisite of his and all his friends' toilettes. It was applied to hats, coats, boots, cravats indiscriminately, and as he added, 'So many of us were poets, there was always plenty of it about.'

Of these men, who were at that time all poor together, some afterwards achieved popularity as well as abundant prosperity; some, equally gifted, failed to obtain recognition, and some, again, fell upon evil days when advanced in life. Stephen Heller, the dreamy composer and sensitive,

---

[1] Garcia, brother of Maria Malibran and Pauline Viardot, lived from 1805 to 1906 and was the greatest singing teacher of his century, numbering Jenny Lind and Charles Santley among his pupils. From 1848 to 1895 he was a professor at the Royal Academy of Music.

nervous man, pushed to one side and neglected in the busy Paris of to-day, was one of these; in addition to other misfortunes he became nearly blind in his old age, and with the loss of his sight lost the means of earning the little that sufficed to support his modest existence. My father, who had maintained the closest intimacy with Heller, became aware of his trouble and felt that this could not, should not be, and that some among the thousands who had enjoyed his music must come forward and save the aged musician from want. A 'Heller Testimonial' was started, and soon enough money was subscribed to purchase a small annuity and enable our dear old friend to end his days in peace. Their correspondence shows the infinite trouble my father took in the matter, not the least part of which was the difficulty of persuading Heller to allow his necessity to be made known.

It may surprise those who know how popular Heller's music has become, especially in England, to learn that it did not bring in an adequate return; but the annals of art are full of similar cases. A picture which may some day fetch thousands at Christie's, a book which may run through many editions, and a song which may be sung all over the country will, as often as not, fail to produce anything for the author or the artist but the most paltry sum. Thus, the 'Wanderstunden', by Heller, which is to be found in the library of every musical amateur, was sold out and out with four other pieces for 15l.!

The prompt sympathy which made my father come forward to the relief of his old comrade is not to be wondered at, but his ready willingness to assist those in want who had no real claim upon him was evinced in a hundred directions. His purse was always open, and in many other ways was he ready to give assistance when needed. A touching evidence of this was given to us many years ago in Manchester, when my father, returning to his house in Greenheys,[1] noticed that the old postman who was in the

[1] No. 70, Greenheys Lane. It was demolished in 1896.

habit of bringing him his letters had evidently been too generously regaled at the houses at which he had already called—it was Christmas time—and was not in a fit condition to deliver the rest of his letters. Knowing that the poor man would be dismissed if his state was discovered or any mistake occurred in the letters entrusted to his care, my father went the rest of his round with him, delivering every letter to its proper address, and, when the bag was quite empty, took the postman home with him and did not let him go until he was quite sober again. It is gratifying to add that the man was exceedingly grateful, never again lapsed from the path of sobriety, and continued on his old beat for some years afterwards.

Cabmen were also great friends of my father's; he got on beautifully with them and they with him, and many an amusing story would he bring home about them, especially after a visit to Dublin. One honest and worthy Jehu evinced his devotion in a very striking manner. At the time of the Franco-Prussian war it was rumoured in Manchester that my father would have to go and serve in the German army, so 'James', for such was his respected name, came to our house one evening and begged to be allowed to take my father's place and go out as his substitute to the seat of war. . .

Nothing . . . took my father away for long from his beloved piano. Wherever he might go for his holidays Messrs. Broadwood would send him one of their big instruments, and much amusement have we had in seeing the whole fisher population of some seaside place turn out to trundle the big case up to the house my father might have taken. Cowes was for many years his favourite holiday resort, at first a cottage at East Cowes, and later Egypt House, West Cowes a delightful place with a garden down to the sea, at that time a school, but my father was able to take it during the holiday months—August and September. Here the piano, with many 'yo-heave-hos' and other nautical sounds, would be installed, and then how

177

delightful it was on hot summer nights to sit in the garden, or on the low wall overhanging the sea, and hear the 'Moonlight' and other divine sonatas played as only my father could play them.

Our dear friend Richard Doyle once wrote, in refusing an invitation to repeat a visit to us there:—

I dare not run away for a day, because I know that once in sight of the sea I should not be able to move from it. And oh! the Schuberts, Hellers, and the moonlight nights, how I wish my eyes and ears were among them.

. . . I do not know how much real musicians are affected by the conditions under which music is heard—whether to them it is a matter of indifference whether they listen to it in a crowded concert room or among surroundings such as I have described above, but as to an artist a picture conveys quite a different expression when seen in the church for which it was painted, or when forming part of the decoration of a beautiful room, from what it does when hung in an auction room, so to a mere amateur do beautiful surroundings and the sympathy of friends enhance the pleasure derived from music.

A house where all these conditions were enjoyed to perfection was that lovely cottage in Kensington, the home of the Prinseps and of Watts, Little Holland House.[1]

Here on Sunday afternoons in summer, men who were famous and women who were beautiful would assemble; croquet and bowls, tea and strawberries, would serve as accompaniments to merry, witty talk, and here at dusk and often far into the night, my father and Joachim would take to their instruments, and convey thoughts of the great masters of their art to the ears of Tennyson and Swinburne, Burne Jones and Rossetti, Watts,[2] Browning, Leighton, Millais, Fred Walker, Doyle, and many another poet and

---

[1] Little Holland House, Melbury Road was demolished in the 1960s.
[2] G. F. Watts's portrait of Hallé is in the National Portrait Gallery.

painter who lingered on to listen to them.

My father always delighted in having such men to play to; with painters, as he has himself said, he was always safe—with *littérateurs* he was occasionally not quite so fortunate. They were fond of talking and found it difficult to sit long and listen, whatever other sounds were being made, and at times matters fared even worse. Some years ago, in 1864, Professor Ruskin asked him to come and play to a school of young girls in whom he was greatly interested. My father readily consented, and as the Professor was there himself, and it was the first time he had played to him, he was careful to select what was most great and beautiful, and played his very best. When it was all over and my father was about to leave, one of the girls told him she had been practising Thalberg's arrangement of 'Home, Sweet Home', and would very much like to hear my father play it before he went away. He told her it was a pity they should listen to a trivial thing like that after the beautiful music they had just heard, but as she appeared disappointed and some other girls came forward with the same request, he gave way, sat down again, and played it. To his chagrin, Ruskin, who had been politely appreciative, now became enthusiastic and told him *that* was the piece he liked best far and away. Of course my father said nothing at the time, but it got to the ears of the Professor how disappointed my father had been, so he wrote him the following letter:—

Winnington Hall, Northwich, Cheshire:

Dec. 3, 1864

Dear Mr. Hallé,—My 'children' tell me you were sorry because I like that 'Home S.H.' better than Beethoven—having expected better sympathy from me. But how could you—with all your knowledge of your art, and of men's minds? Believe me, you *cannot* have sympathy from any untaught person, respecting the higher noblenesses of composition. If I were with you a year, you could make me feel them—I am quite capable of doing so, were I taught—but

179

the utmost you ought *ever* to hope from a musically-illiterate person is honesty and modesty. I do not—should not—expect you to sympathise with *me* about a bit of Titian, but I know that you would, if I had a year's teaching of you, and I know that you would never tell me you liked it, or *fancy* you liked it, to please me.

But I want to tell you, nevertheless, *why* I liked that H. S. H. I do *not* care about the air of it, I have no doubt it is what you say it is—sickly and shallow. But I did care about hearing a million of low notes in perfect cadence and succession of sweetness. I never recognised before so many notes in a given brevity of moment, all sweet and helpful. I have often heard glorious harmonies and inventive and noble succession of harmonies, but *i* never in my life heard a variation like that.

Also, I had not before been close enough to see your hands, and the invisible velocity was wonderful to me, quite unspeakably, merely as a human power.

You must not therefore think I only cared for the bad music—but it is quite true that I don't understand Beethoven, and I fear I never shall have time to learn to do so.

Forgive me this scrawl, and let me talk with you again, some day.

Ever with sincere regards to Mrs. and Miss Hallé, gratefully and respectfully yours,

J. RUSKIN

There was perhaps one further reason for my being so much struck with that. I had heard Thalberg play it after the Prussian Hymn. I had gone early that I might sit close to him, and I was entirely disappointed, it made no impression on me whatever. Your variation therefore took me with greater and singular surprise.

On commenting on this letter my father never would admit that he could not appreciate Titian without instruction, and he had such a genuine love for pictures and such a good eye that I felt with him the Professor had failed to prove his case.

180

. . . There was one social gathering which he would never miss if he could possibly help it, and that was Sir Frederick Leighton's annual party in the spring. He dearly liked playing in a studio and among pictures, and one of the dreams of his life was to found an institution where the two arts should work in harmony together.

When the Grosvenor Gallery was started and I was appointed one of the directors he thought his opportunity had come, and for one or two seasons he gave concerts of chamber music in the gallery; but as his recitals had formerly been always held in the afternoon, the change of hour to the evening caused much disappointment among his regular subscribers, many of whom were students at musical colleges; so the Grosvenor concerts had to be abandoned, and the venue changed to the Prince's or St. James's Hall.

Concerts and recitals have become a matter of such every-day occurrence in London nowadays, and so many pianists of amazing skill arrive here each season, that my father no longer saw the necessity of continuing his recitals regularly every summer, and of late years they were somewhat interrupted. It was, however, his intention to give a farewell series of pianoforte recitals during the coming spring (1896), in order to play all the Beethoven sonatas once again in consecutive order, and he had already fixed the dates and taken the St. James's Hall for the purpose. With what devotion he would have accomplished this final act of homage to the genius of the hero in whose service he had spent his life, only those able in some degree to measure the depth of his reverence for him can form any idea. With the music of a Beethoven concerto he first appealed to English ears more than half a century ago, and in the quiet of his study, the room he loved best, which he always quitted with regret and returned to with eager pleasure, within the twenty-four last hours of his life, he sat playing a Beethoven concerto almost within the shadow of death.

181

From 1869 onwards my father's recitals had ceased to be concerts for pianoforte alone, concerted chamber music being regularly introduced as well as an occasional vocal piece. The artists most constantly associated with him were Mme. Norman Neruda, Herr Straus, and Signor Piatti, and among the many works introduced by him for the first time in England were trios, quartets, and quintets by Brahms, Dvořák, Saint-Saëns, and other modern composers. . .

In 1880 my father brought out a work at his orchestral concerts in Manchester, the production of which gave him the greatest pleasure and interest; this was Berlioz's 'Faust'. The Hungarian March and the 'Ballet des Sylphes' were well known, as they had often been given at previous concerts; but to give the work in its entirety had been my father's ambition for years, and he at last ventured on it in spite of the doubts expressed by many of his friends as to its proving a popular success. The concert excited much interest throughout England, and many well-known musicians repaired to Manchester to hear the first performance of a work which had been so much discussed, and about which so many contrary opinions were held.

The performance, which had been preceded by many careful rehearsals, was at all points magnificent, and reflected the greatest credit upon both band and chorus, whilst the principal vocalists, Miss Mary Davies, Mr. Lloyd, Mr. Hilton, and Mr. Henschel rendered the solos admirably. The work was received with so much enthusiasm that my father gave it a second time during the same season, a very rare proceeding on his part. Indeed, it is worthy of note that during the thirty-eight years' existence of the Manchester concerts, this compliment has only been paid to the following great choral works:—Handel's 'Messiah', of which a double performance takes place every Christmas; Handel's 'Jephtha', owing to the remarkable success of Mr. Sims Reeves in 1868; Gluck's

'Iphigenia', given three times in the course of 1860; and the music to the 'Midsummer Night's Dream', by Mendelssohn, given twice in the season of 1857–58.

The following year, 1881, my father took his band and chorus to London and gave a performance of 'Faust' at St. James's Hall, the soloists being the same as in Manchester. Again the *chef d'oeuvre* of Berlioz was received with acclamation, and both here and in Manchester it has been repeated over and over again with ever increasing popularity, whilst in nearly all the greater towns of England it has been performed with the utmost success.

I went to Manchester for the first performance of 'Faust', and being anxious to know something about it before the concert took place in the evening I attended the rehearsal. A little incident occurred which revealed to me my father's wonderful accuracy of ear, and which I may be pardoned for repeating. In the second part of 'Faust', when the hero of the legend meets his doom and is consigned to the infernal regions, there occurs an interlude for the orchestra expressive of the exultation felt by the denizens of hell over their latest victim. When I first heard this piece I felt inclined to think my father had given *carte blanche* to every member of his band to make any noise he liked, provided it was loud and of a horrible nature.

When it was over, what was my astonishment to hear my father quietly say: 'The second clarinet played an E flat instead of an E natural in the eighth bar. I hope he will take care not to do so at the concert this evening!'

Musicians may possibly scoff at this anecdote, and say that it is only what any good conductor would have done; but, as I said at the beginning of this chapter, I have no knowledge of music, only a great love for it, and an absolute faith that the manner in which it was presented to me by my father, whether in his playing on the piano or his conducting of his orchestra, was the best of all. Many pianists had greater executive skill, as he was the first to admit, but none had his absolute forgetfulness of self, none,

I think, so limpid and liquid a touch when translating into sound the thoughts of the master whose score he had before him.

This quickness of perception and clearness of expression were part of his character as a man, and were as remarkable in his speech as in his rendering of music; no one was ever left for a moment in doubt as to what he meant, and I think it was this gift which made even the most difficult music intelligible to the unlearned when my father was at the piano or in the conductor's chair.

At the end of one of his concerts the remarks overheard were not so often 'How splendidly Hallé played,' or 'How wonderfully he conducted,' as 'How beautiful was that sonata,' or 'How glorious that symphony'; and I think that was the highest tribute that could be paid him, and the one which his modest nature and single-minded devotion to his art most appreciated.

Another gift my father possessed, and which never failed to fill me with astonishment, was his marvellous memory. A piece of music once read or heard seemed to be indelibly imprinted on some portion of his brain, and was there at his command whenever he wanted it. A remarkable instance of this occurred some years ago when Stephen Heller was here on a visit to us. He and my father had been talking about the evening on which the Revolution of 1848 broke out—how they heard the first shots fired as they went for a stroll together before parting for the night, and this naturally led them to recall the stirring events of the next few months, events sufficiently exciting and momentous to them both to obliterate, as one would have thought, all the incidents of the quiet evening they had spent together on that fateful night before they heard the firing. Presently Heller said to my father: 'Do you remember, Hallé, that I had composed a little sonata on that day, and when you came to me in the evening I asked you to play it to me? I wonder if you could play it to me now.' 'Good gracious!' said my father, 'I have never given it a thought from that day to this, but I'll try,' and he sat down at the piano and played it through without the mistake of a single note!

In spite of his unfailing memory he would often play, but would never conduct, without having the score before him. He maintained that to give an exhibition of his memory was not part of the programme of the concert, and that however perfect his recollection of a symphony or other concerted piece might be, he had greater command over his band when he could give all his attention to the proper rendering of the work they were about, without being distracted by any exercise of memory; yet when occasion demanded, his power of playing and conducting by heart never failed him, and very useful at times did it prove. Once, when about to go on the platform to play the Kreutzer Sonata with Lady Hallé, he discovered that the music had been left at home. 'Never mind,' he said; 'let's play it without,' and they went through it without a wrong note.

My father's excellent memory was not confined to music. It combined with a love of accuracy and order, and that power of calculation, so often accompanying the musical gift, which he possessed in a high degree, to make him a splendid man of business.

From the early part of October to the middle of March he had to make, year after year, arrangements for from two to five concerts every week, some in Manchester, others in different parts of England, Scotland, or Ireland. These concerts were either orchestral, when his whole band accompanied him, or recitals of chamber music, where the performers were Lady Hallé and himself. The correspondence, the business arrangements, the selection of programmes for all these different towns, and the care that had to be taken not to give the various audiences the same piece twice over within a given time, involved an enormous amount of work, and yet my father never kept a secretary, and had every detail of this vast business so clearly in his head that he was never at fault, and would often send his agents instructions about financial arrangements, programmes, &c., when he was on a journey away from his letters and note-books.

The quickness with which he despatched his correspondence always filled his family with astonishment. He would sit down to his study-table with a pile of letters before him, yet in an incredibly short time they were all disposed of. His system was to answer, or file for reference, each letter as it came, before he opened the next, and however hurried he might be, he never showed in his handwriting, which was faultlessly clear and beautiful, nor in what he wrote, any sign of haste. His business letters were models of conciseness, with never a word too many or too few, while he seemed to have an equal facility in expressing himself in English, French, or German.

He would probably with his business capacities have been very successful financially as well as artistically in all his undertakings had not his artist's temperament run away with him whenever it became a question of money being weighed in the balance against music. Music was his goddess, who had always to be decked in the richest raiment, and all other considerations vanished in face of the primary aim of making his concerts as good as money could make them. He would calculate the expenses and receipts with the greatest facility, and audit his accounts to the fraction of a penny; but whether the balance was to or against his credit was always a matter of comparative indifference so long as the concert had gone well. This and a large-hearted generosity led him to live up to his income without much thought for the future, though he was singularly simple in his habits and content with very little. . .

My father was a man of so much energy and activity of mind that idleness was irksome to him in the last degree. His form of rest from work was to take up some other pursuit. . . He was a great reader, and it is astonishing how much he read considering the number of hours he gave each day to his work. Unlike his friend Heller, whose thoughts always dwelt on the past and whose favourite author was Horace, my father with his strong vitality and love of life lived in the present day and with authors who were his contemporaries. Books of travel and adventure, the history of this and of the latter half of the last century, works of fiction by living French and English writers, the topics of the day and the latest discoveries in science—all interested him greatly.

In religion he was a Catholic, the faith of his first wife, my mother, who died in 1866; of his second wife, Wilhelmina Norman-Neruda, widow of L. Norman of Stockholm, whom he married in 1888; and of the nine children his first wife gave him, eight of whom are still living.

In politics he was a staunch Conservative, but I regret to say his interest was never keen enough to overcome his objection to recording his votes at election times. He somehow connected polling-booths with jury-boxes, and thought if he did his duty as a citizen in the former capacity he might be called upon to serve in the latter, to which he had a particular objection. He thought too by remaining quietly at home when a parliamentary election was going on, the officer whose business it is to collect jurymen would forget his existence and leave him alone, and whatever grounds he had for building up this theory it certainly is a fact that only once was he ever called upon to serve on a jury. I shall never forget his consternation when he received his summons, but his friend the Lord Chief Justice, Sir Alexander Cockburn, to whom he at once repaired in his trouble, arranged matters for him and got him off, and I think must have asked that his name should be taken off the list of possible jurymen permanently, as he was never called upon to serve again either in London or in Manchester. . .

My father was a great respecter of law and constituted authority and desired to be at peace with all men; he had many friends and but few enemies, except amongst those to whom all success in their fellow men is a source of dislike and enmity. He was slow to anger, but when his wrath was roused he was, I am bound to say, a very hard hitter. Criticism on his own account he cared nothing about, but woe to the luckless wight who threw a stone at one of his gods in his presence, and who, to glorify some modern composer, would decry one of the great masters of the art of music. My father had a fine command of words which his great knowledge, unfailing memory, and accuracy, enabled him to use with much effect, and would reduce even the most truculent adversary to silence in a very short time. I used to love to be present at one of these encounters, but they were rare: 'peace and goodwill to all men' might have been his motto through life, and I am sure even his opponents soon forgot and forgave what was never meant in malice.

Of the many proofs of friendship and esteem, public and private, which my father received, I do not think that any, not even his knighthood, conferred in 1887, gave him so much pleasure as the doctor's degree conferred upon him at Edinburgh. He had the robes made for him, sat to me for his portrait in them, and expressed a wish that he might be buried in them—a wish which, needless to say, was piously observed by us when the sad time came for giving effect to it. H.M. the Queen was always very kind to my father and showed him many marks of her favour; he was often bidden to Windsor, Balmoral, and Osborne, to play to her and to the late Prince Consort and to give instruction or to play 'à quatre mains' with her daughters. The Princess of Wales was also a pupil of my father's, and one for whom he had the greatest regard, as her talent was considered by him of a very high order. Both Her Royal Highness and the Prince of Wales treated my father with great affection and friendship, and he was often a guest at Sandringham and Marlborough House. . .

Music, in which my father may be said to have been born, which was his ruling passion through life and in which he died—as he carried his work on to within a few hours of his death—was to him something more than an art: it was a sacred mission. He believed that music, which from all time has accompanied man in his strongest moments of joy and sorrow, which stirs him to deeds of courage and is his ultimate expression of love and praise, is a force for good, which cannot be gainsaid. He believed, as all lovers of music believe, that it is above the power of words in its influence on the spiritual side of man's nature, and that many a heart has been stirred to a sense of what is good and beautiful through music which otherwise might have gone through life unconscious that such things are. It was this faith that made my father's work of such absorbing interest to him, and which made him choose as the field of his labour those busy manufacturing towns of the north of England, where men's lives are spent in work—too often mere monotonous drudgery, and amid surroundings of dirt and ugliness such as the world has never seen before. To these grimy workers, to these makers of ships and of guns, of engines and of fabrics, whose ears were wearied by the ceaseless noise of machinery, he brought the strains of the most exquisite music ever heard by man, and made them forget, if but for a few minutes, the office and the workshop, and remember that existence has other things to offer. This was my father's life and work for nearly fifty years spent in England. He may have had a mistaken idea of the power of music and overrated the importance of it as a refining influence in men's lives, but he acted from the highest of all motives, and the work he did he did thoroughly and well.

On the morning of Friday, October 25, 1895, after a few hours' illness, he passed peacefully away. *Requiescat in pace.*

Letters

[Translated from the German]

Greenheys, Manchester:
October 22, 1858

My dear Mother—It seems incredible, but it is none the less true, that only the desire of writing fully and at great length, to tell you how happy I was during my stay with you, and with what pleasure I think of the too short time spent with you, has been the very cause of my not writing at all. . .

I found all my family in the best condition on my return, strengthened and invigorated by sea-bathing; the little ones had much to tell of donkey rides and other pleasures, and they amuse us often with their very comical recollections. They have now got used to their Manchester life again, and are all working hard at their lessons. In what concerns my own business, I found the time I had allowed myself for preparation for my first concert, which took place on September 15, all too short; my whole orchestra had to be re-organised, and I have really had not a minute's rest. Besides this, the new choral society, of which I had laid the foundations before my departure, had to be brought to completion, and in this I have got so far that its first concert, Haydn's 'Creation', takes place this very day, with the unheard of number of 1,600 subscribers, and an orchestra and chorus of 300. I have just come home from the very satisfactory final rehearsal, and am full of expectation for this evening. My chamber music concerts will recommence on November 25, the St. Cecilia in a fortnight, *und so geht der alte Trödel wieder los.* . .

[To his wife Désirée; translated from the French]

London: May 3, 1859

Yesterday I first rehearsed with Wieniawski; then, at Joachim's, I assisted at the rehearsal of the Beethoven quartets that he is to play on Wednesday; it was magnificent, I have rarely had a greater treat. It gave me such a rage for work that

190

I practised from dinner-time until one o'clock in the morning and wish I could begin again to-day.

Glasgow: February 1, 1860

There were a great many people yesterday, in a charming room that I had not seen before . . . everything went well. The concert ended with the Kreutzer sonata, after which we were thrown a bouquet, which we both looked at with no little astonishment. As Vieuxtemps did not budge, I picked it up and offered it to him before the public, but he would not accept it; then I went bravely into the artists' room, and I gave it to—- Madame Vieuxtemps.

Monday

Only two words to-day; I have three lessons to give, another rehearsal this evening, and I must work again at that wretched English music that is not worth a rap, and yet is incredibly difficult. It is really a pity to give oneself so much trouble about things that certainly are not worth it—but how can one refuse to play at an *English* concert in London? I should have been drawn and quartered, at the least, by the *Times* . . . I shall arrive on Wednesday afternoon, and I have asked D. to change the rehearsal from Friday to Thursday, as I shall probably have to leave again on Thursday evening.

Baden-Baden, August 17, 1860,
Hôtel de Hollande

I have been at Baden since yesterday; the weather was magnificent when I left Heidelberg, which helped me to decide, and I have met here Berlioz, Richard Wagner, Danton, Sivori, Wolff, Cossmann, Piatti, and several other old acquaintances. I spent nearly the whole day yesterday with Berlioz; we went through the score of 'Armida', and, from memory, the whole of 'Iphigenia', and I learned many things that I was ignorant of and which he knows by tradition. He showed me effects that I should never have discovered by myself. I am therefore very pleased to have seen him. I am writing in P.'s room, whom I met this morning . . . We have just had a long talk about the Manchester Theatre; he is more than ever convinced of the possibility of the scheme, and thinks it would be a good thing for Manchester and for me.

Paris: August 19, 1860,
Hotel du Louvre

. . . I also met at Baden Mme. Miolan and her husband, and Wieniawski with his wife; moreover, I assisted at the rehearsal of a grand concert, which Berlioz conducted, where he rehearsed a great part of 'Orpheus', which interested me keenly; I again learned many effects that I did not know before. Poor Berlioz, however, gave me the greatest pain; I never saw a man so changed, and, but for a miracle, he will surely be in his grave before this time next year. He knows it himself, and speaks of it with a sadness that pierces one's heart. He was so pleased to see me and to be able to open his heart in talking of music; he told me he had not felt so well for a long time as during those two days. . . .

I am now going to hunt for Heller, I hope he is in Paris; this evening I intend to go and hear 'Fra Diavolo' at the Opéra Comique, unless Heller has something else to propose.

Royal Hotel, Princes Street, Edinburgh:
Sunday ('61 ?)

Yesterday's concert was a great success, and I shall have 601. for my share, which makes it worth while; the public was truly admirable, and all the aristocracy for forty miles around was there. The duchess was very sorry that I could not go to Dalkeith, but she hopes that another time I can arrange to spend a week there.

The X.'s had invited about a score of people for the evening, so that I had to play a little, in spite of my fatigue, and to swallow a dozen Scotch ballads. There was a Mrs. ——, who made me spend one of the most terrible quarters of an hour that I can remember for a long time; imagine an oldish woman, very extraordinary in attire, with a bass voice like that of Formes, who stands up, alone, in the middle of the room and, without any accompaniment, sings to improvised melodies with all sorts of old-fashioned shakes and hiccoughs, several of her brother's poems, and by no means the shortest of them. I was seized with such a fear of bursting into laughter that it nearly made me ill.

[From Stephen Heller; translated from the French]

Paris: December 5, 1861

My dear Hallé—Your letter gave me very great pleasure—I might say, joy. First of all I shall obtain what I desired, and then it is to your friendship and to your exertions that I shall owe this realisation of my wishes. I thank you, dear friend, very sincerely for having made use of your position and of your influence in favour of your old comrade. What you tell me of the solidity of the house of Chappell tranquillises me. . . . You know me well enough to be assured that I am not a man who looks for gain. Nevertheless, I ought to tell you that it is not for myself that I desire to earn a little of that vile metal that is so necessary. For several years I have had to support several members of my family who had lost their all. But, with my compositions, especially if I succeed in getting better remuneration in Paris (as, thanks to you, is already the case in England), and with some pupils who would pay me well, I could manage. I have obtained a good result only in Germany, where the publishers of all parts wish to have my works. If I had an artist of your quality here I should have done equally well. But it is always the same old story. I divide artists and amateurs into three categories on this head. The first play my things well—this is but a small category; the second play them badly and are far more numerous; the third do not play them at all, and are the most numerous of all. Yes, there are a few who play some of my pieces well. A few professors, a few little girls, who play very fast above all things, and a few amateurs, who like Chopin, Schumann, Mendelssohn, and who do me the honour to let me follow these masters. But all these are not very animated, nor simple enough, nor ornate enough, or they are simple where they ought to be ornate, and ornate where they ought to be simple; sentimental where they should be warm and tender; powerful instead of amiable, heavy in light passages, and *vice versa*. You have remained my ideal of a pianist, for you never exaggerate. That is where one recognises the master in every art. You are never emphatic (a horrid thing in any manifestation of art), bombastic, whimpering, affected; for you neither wish to make rocks weep, nor to tame wild beasts, nor to move mountains; you have *true* sentiment, and that is everything. I sum up everything in that. The great writers, the great painters had *true* sentiment, nothing more and nothing less. The artist who goes beyond, and he who stops short of it have equally missed their aim. I hold modern pianists in horror while recognising their great qualities. But these qualities, what do they amount to? Of a truth, I have not heard them play the easiest of Beethoven's sonatas in a manner to content me, to give me the composer's meaning. The *great* Rubinstein played several 'Waldstücke' at my house (the one in E among others). What a style! What exaggeration of the less salient parts, and what negligence in the more important passages! One felt the boredom of those agile and powerful fingers that had nothing put into them, as when they give the circus elephant an empty salad-bowl to swallow. He played my Tarantelle in A flat at St. Petersburg, ornamented with octave passages, shakes, &c., &c. If such people only dared they would do the same to Beethoven.

Stephen Heller

[To a Manchester newspaper]

February 13, 1862
The remarks of your musical critic on yesterday's concert must lead your readers to believe that the introduction of 'Cadenzas' into Mozart's concertos is optional with the performer.[1] I feel sure you will allow me to remove such an impression, and to inform the writer of the paragraph as well as your readers that in all concertos by Mozart, in five out of the six written by Beethoven, and in almost every other instance (Mendelssohn excepted), 'Cadenzas', the place for which is distinctly marked and prepared for in a peculiar manner known to all musicians, cannot be dispensed with without destroying the symmetry of the work, or involving its mutilation. It is hardly necessary to explain that the object of these 'Cadenzas' is to recapitulate the

---

[1] Heller and Hallé had played the E flat concerto for two pianofortes (K.365).

principal ideas contained in the movement, at the conclusion of which they are introduced; to condense them, present them in a new form, and, in short, to give a *résumé* of the whole work. That this has perhaps in no instance on record been done in a more masterly manner than by Mr. Stephen Heller yesterday, all musicians at the concert will readily acknowledge.

Far from being an 'intrusion', or a violation of 'the principle which demands respect for the creations of genius,' the composition of 'Cadenzas' is therefore in strict accordance with the intentions of our greatest composers, and has always been regarded as one of the severest tests of the musician's faculties.

Thanking you for the space you have kindly allowed me, I remain, yours very obediently,

Charles Hallé

[To his wife; translated from the French]

London: March 26, 1863

I have at this moment (10 p.m.) arrived from Windsor, and I will relate my adventures before going to bed. I arrived there at two o'clock; Ruland had an excellent luncheon ready in his room, during which he told me that we should go up to the Rubens room afterwards (where there are two pianos) to make a little music, and that we should perhaps receive a visit from the Princess of Wales, who had known for the last two days, through Lady Augusta Bruce, that I was expected to-day. A little after three o'clock we went upstairs and began to play duets. Presently a servant came in with a little note from Lady A. Bruce to Ruland, to tell him that the Lord Mayor's deputation, &c., &c., had arrived so late that they had put an end to the Princess's intention of coming to hear us. I was naturally a little disappointed, and yet pleased that the Princess had thought of me. After another quarter of an hour Lady Augusta Bruce came in and was graciousness itself; she is a very amiable lady, passionately fond of music. I had to play a sonata of Schubert's, one of Beethoven's, and heaven knows how many little pieces by Bach, Mendelssohn, Heller, &c. She only left us at past six o'clock, and then we went back to Ruland's room. We were

195

hardly there when a servant came in with the agreeable message: 'The Prince and Princess of Wales wish to see Mr. Hallé.' We went in all haste to the private apartments (Ruland to present me), and as we were waiting at the door to be announced, Princess Alice and Prince Louis, who had evidently also been sent for, passed us to go into the Prince's room. Princess Alice stopped and shook hands with me very affectionately, saying it was a very long time since she had last seen me. A moment later, we followed her in, and the Prince of Wales, after shaking hands cordially, presented me to his wife, of whose beauty and grace the photographs give no idea. There was no one present but the Prince and Princess of Wales, Princess Alice and Prince Louis, Ruland and I, and I stayed until half-past seven o'clock, either making music, or joining in familiar and most agreeable conversation upon all manner of subjects. The Prince of Wales asked me to buy him three pianos, two grands, the best that I could find, for his house, 'one for downstairs, and the other for upstairs,' as he said, and the third, a cottage piano in 'maple wood and green silk', which he means to give to Princess Alice. When at last we were dismissed he called Ruland back, just as I was going out, to ask him if I was going to London this season for any length of time, and when Ruland told him I was there already and meant to stay, he said: 'Ah, I am very glad.' It seems evident, therefore, that the Princess means to ask me to give her lessons, or that the Prince has some intentions concerning me, or he would never have asked me to buy him three pianos. Ruland and Becker are of the same opinion, and greatly pleased, I assure you. I am further advanced than Becker, for he has not yet spoken to the Princess of Wales, whereas I have sat beside her for an hour. So my day was not wasted; may this account of it give you pleasure.

[To one of his daughters]

Osborne: December 28, 1866

I will only report shortly the events of the day, as Sahl promises that you will receive this letter on Sunday morning; there is no chance of your getting one to-morrow. I got to London at six in the morning, having slept a few hours in the railway carriage between Crewe and Rugby, and reached Cowes about a quarter past three, where I found the excellent Sahl at the landing place (East Cowes) waiting for me. He took me at once to Osborne, where I am still; on the way we met the Queen driving with Princess Helena, who both bowed and smiled most graciously. At Osborne I found an excellent luncheon prepared for me in Sahl's room, saw Sir John Cowell who manages the household, and was informed by him that I was to have General Grey's apartments (not in the Palace, thank Heaven, but in the first house near the big gate); everybody was very polite, and at five o'clock I received the message that the Queen wished to see me at half-past five. I had, therefore, to go to her just as I was, there being no time to go back to General Grey's house; fortunately Sahl lent me a clean collar, mine being rather dirty from travelling. At half-past five I was ushered into a small boudoir, and after a minute the Queen, Princesses Helena, Louise, and Beatrice, and Prince Leopold came in, were also awfully kind and polite, made me play lots of things, and kept me till seven o'clock. The thing was extremely interesting and agreeable, but I shall tell you all about it on my return. Sahl had ordered dinner for us two in his room, in order to avoid dressing, but to-morrow I shall have breakfast, &c., with the household. Between luncheon and the visit to the Queen Prince Leopold came to fetch me to his room, where we were as jolly as two larks. I must add that there was not a single attendant with the Royalties all the time I was with them, which made it all the more pleasant. What is going to happen to-morrow I do not know, except that breakfast is at half-past nine.

[To his daughter Louise]

Osborne: December 29, 1866

My dear Louise . . . I have given M. an account of yesterday, so I may go on with to-day's events. Between breakfast and luncheon, after I had written a few letters in order to substitute the 'Elijah' for 'Iphigenia' on the 10th, Sahl and I went out for a walk as far as West Cowes, stepped on board the Queen's yacht for a few minutes, and had a look at the American yachts, which are rather ugly. . .

197

After luncheon, Sahl being busy, I went with Baron v. Schroeter (who has the little Prussian prince in charge[1]) down to the shore in the grounds to have another look at the American yachts, which came there that the Queen might have a look at them, and to salute her. The Queen, with a large party, was also at the water's edge, but we, of course, kept aloof. At half-past four o'clock we turned in again, at five your letter came, and I had just opened the envelope when I was called to the Queen; I saw her, with all her children, in the same room as yesterday, and remained till about half-past six o'clock; nothing could be pleasanter, except that I had rather too much to play. Once more in Sahl's room I took your letter out of my pocket to read it, when a message came from Princess Helena, or rather Princess Christian, as she is now called, if I would be kind enough to come and see her in her room. So off I trotted again, and after a little chat she asked if I would play a few duets with her, or if I was too tired? Of course we set to work again, and it was five minutes to eight when she gave me leave to go; there was just time to dress, and your letter had actually to wait till after dinner before I could at last read it. The Queen takes most kindly to music; she has suggested many of the pieces I played, and now I am no longer anxious about the choice, but may play just what suits me.

Altogether this is an extraordinary visit, but when shall I get away from here? there is the rub; the Queen speaks, and Princess Helena speaks as if I were going to stop here for ever. . .

December 31, 1866

I am not to leave Osborne before Wednesday morning, the Queen wishing to see me again this afternoon at half-past five o'clock, to spend the evening with the Duchess of Athole and the other ladies (perhaps the Princesses), and to play to her, for the last time, to-morrow evening after dinner instead of this evening.

So I cannot be at the rehearsal on Wednesday evening, and this makes me as busy as a bee, writing to D. and arranging matters. . . . I shall now arrive on Wednesday night between two and three o'clock, and reserve all further news till then; this

---

[1] Later Kaiser Wilhelm II.

is a visit which the Queen is sure not to forget, and it will keep me in her good graces for ever.

[From Robert Browning]

19 Warwick Crescent,
Upper Westbourne Terrace, W.:
May 14, 1867

My dear Hallé—All thanks for your invitation, which I shall profit by if I possibly can.

I want to explain to you why in all probability I shall be away from your music[1] for once; it is foolish, I know. My son goes to college at Michaelmas and has to work so hard in order to matriculate at Balliol, where he wants to go, that he *cannot* spare even one morning a week, and I have got so used to have him with me that I can't bear sitting alone. Next year, if all goes well with us both, I shall assuredly do the nearly one thing I thoroughly enjoy now. Ever yours truly,

Robert Browning

[From Stephen Heller; translated from the French]

Paris: December 3, 1874

My dear Hallé—Your letter gave me great pleasure, and you have rendered me a signal service by introducing me to an honest publisher—*rara avis. . .*

Wagner's sonata is idiotic.[2] One is all the more astonished at the immense transformation of the man. When can he have written this sample of grocery? One would say that when he wrote it he did not know, I will not say Beethoven, but even one sonata of Hummel's, Dussek's, or even Kalkbrenner's, who has given us some pretty specimens in this style. The latter, at any rate, knew the piano.

When one comes away from a fine performance of an opera, or the perfect execution of a symphony, one likes to recall the pleasure by going through the score on the piano. This I did after

[1] Hallé's piano recitals at St James's Hall.
[2] Presumably the B flat pianoforte sonata of 1832.

hearing you play Chopin's 'Nocturne' and 'Barcarolle'. I had never judged these two works according to their value. I had rarely heard them, and incompletely, and I had never been tempted to read them myself, being frightened by the difficulties they represent. Your truly incomparable execution entirely modified my opinion. So interpreted, one recognises their great merit, their great value; they are worthy of Chopin. For the hundredth time I lamented over the disastrous position of works of music. They remain a dead-letter unless they can find a great artist of good-will, who takes upon himself the task of making them understood and liked.

The painter has no need of an interpreter. A frame and daylight are sufficient for him.

According to your letter you must be at this moment among valleys and mountains. Do not work too hard, do not become too rich, and try, from time to time, to give your best friend another Sunday like the last in Paris. Your old

Stephen Heller

[To his daughter Marie]

Vienna: October 9, 1880

Dearest M—I cannot remember having spent more interesting days than these last few ones. Brahms is the most delightful and good-natured creature imaginable, and what a musician! He knows everything, has everything in his library, and seems quite happy when he can talk about musical curiosities, or about works and certain points in works, which must interest every musician. We have dined together every day at the coffee house ('Der Igel') where Beethoven used to dine, spent a few hours afterwards in talk, met again in the evening and remained together till midnight.

Then I have made the acquaintance of Pohl, the author of a most remarkable biography of Haydn, and keeper of the musical archives here; he is a charming, warm-hearted man, and has shown me all his treasures, autographs without number, and such interesting ones! MS. scores of Beethoven's, Mozart's, Haydn's, Bach's Symphonies, Concertos, unpublished works even; it would have been worth my while to remain months in those rooms.

Nottebohm[1] is another remarkable man and writer on musical matters, who is in possession of the most curious MS. sketches of Beethoven's sonatas, which have helped me to decide several doubtful passages in some of them, about which I have often quarrelled with Bülow and others. Richter, Helmesberger, Brüll, Hanslick,[2] and many others, are all delightful people, and I feel very sorry that go I must on Monday. The weather is delightful into the bargain.

[To his daughters Mathilde and Nora]

Leipzig, Hotel Hauffe: October 14, 1880

Dearest M. and N.—

. . . My stay in Vienna has been wonderfully interesting; Brahms has taken to me like a duck to the water (of which I feel not a little proud); he hardly ever left me, and on Monday afternoon even went to the station—a very long way indeed—to see me off. I shall have a deal to tell when I am once back in London.

I left Vienna on Monday at 2.10 P.M., and arrived here on Tuesday morning shortly after seven. Yesterday morning at nine o'clock I had the rehearsal, which went off very well, and to-night at half-past six is the concert, which I wish was over already. I play a Beethoven Concerto and several small pieces by Chopin; at the rehearsal the audience (there is rather a large one at the rehearsals here) was very *perlite* to me; nevertheless, I am a little nervous just now. The band, I am happy to say, is not quite equal to our Manchester band; that is a fact.

Yesterday evening I saw the celebrated 'Meiningen' actors in Shakespeare's 'Winter's Tale'; they certainly play wonderfully well without having any really great actors; it is the perfection of 'ensemble', and very striking.

To-morrow, early, I am off for Dresden, where I play on

---

[1] Martin Gustav Nottebohm (1817-82), composer and writer whose investigation of Beethoven's sketchbooks was a masterpiece of research.

[2] Hans Richter, who conducted the first Bayreuth *Ring*, later succeeded Hallé in Manchester; Joseph Helmesberger was director of the Vienna Conservatory and leader of a famous string quartet; Eduard Hanslick was the Vienna critic noted for his championship of Brahms and his antipathy to Wagner.

Saturday evening, quite alone, with only a few songs. On Sunday evening I shall be at Hagen, where I must remain a few days, and I shall reach London on Thursday evening next, or perhaps on Friday, to go off to Manchester, on Saturday, the first concert taking place on Monday, the 25th.

[To his daughter Marie]

Vienna: Hotel Imperial,
April 2, 1881

Dearest M—So I have at last played in Vienna, and may say that I have every reason to be pleased. I played Beethoven's Concerto in E flat and three pieces by Chopin, and after each performance I was recalled five times to the platform. People are very complimentary, and if we were not so near Easter I might certainly play again; as it is, I may be sure to be welcomed another time. At Prague, three days ago, I was even recalled seven times as a rule, and had a great mind to take a chair and sit down on the platform for greater convenience. Here the calls do not mean an 'encore', they are merely complimentary.

Greenheys: October 23, 1881

My dear M—The Huddersfield Festival was really a great success, and the people most enthusiastic. 'Faust' never went so well yet. Lloyd certainly sang better than ever, and so did Miss Davies; Santley was splendid too, although a little fatigued at first. . . .

I send you two Huddersfield and one Bradford papers, which will tell you the whole story. How things grow! I cannot help thinking now often of the evening when I asked you if you could not help me by translating 'Faust', and now people have actually come from Ireland to Huddersfield merely to hear it. I have seen them with my own eyes. They had been ruefully sea-sick, and said they would not mind being so again the next day if they could hear 'Faust' once more.

11 Mansfield Street: August 29, 1882

. . . Yesterday I went to Birmingham to hear a rehearsal of Gounod's 'Redemption'—not a very beautiful work—and came back in the evening to have an interview to-day with Grove. I had found a letter here from him informing me that the Prince of Wales offered me the professorship of the first pianoforte class in the Royal College, and I had to show him by my engagement-books how impossible it was for me to accept. He understood at once, and was sorry. They mean to open next year.

I return to Birmingham this evening, in time for the concert, at which a new work by Benedict—'Graziella'—is to be given. It seems that he fainted the other day at the rehearsal, in spite of which he insists upon conducting it himself.

Gounod was very nice and kissed me, *à la française*, which I thought unnecessary. Gade is there also, and it is altogether an interesting meeting. Poor Costa looks awful, but gets through his work in spite of his illness; there is indomitable pluck in the old fellow.

August 31, 1882

Since I wrote last I have been to Birmingham and heard the first performance of Gounod's 'Redemption'. My first impression was more than confirmed; it is a dull work and monotonous in the extreme. . . .

Yesterday evening I came on to Preston, where everything is in confusion, the Duke of Albany being too ill to make his promised visit.

Bull and Royal Hotel, Preston:[1]
September 7, 1882

Dearest M— . . . I was most happy to read your description of your excursions to Caprile and Agordo, and could not help reading the whole letter to Straus. It must have been delightful.

I cannot say as much for Preston, although the weather has become fine since yesterday. First of all, I have caught a horrid cold, and, secondly, I have to deal with a committee that makes many mistakes in the management, and none of us derive any pleasure from the concerts. Just imagine that the performance of 'Elijah' was announced to commence at half-past eight

---

[1] On the occasion of the Preston Guild Festival.

o'clock—certainly an unreasonably late hour—but the doors could not be *opened* to the public before *a quarter past nine*, because the hall was not ready! You can fancy the row that was going on. We began the performance at 9.30, whilst the people were streaming in, and, of course, for a long time not a note could be heard, much to our disgust. We had not finished until past midnight, in spite of having made no interval.

Yesterday's concert began at the equally stupid hour of 4.30 o'clock, and we ended in perfect darkness, no arrangements having been made for lighting the gas. The crowds of roughs, through which we have to fight our way to and from the concerts, always on foot, are most unsavoury. The processions seem remarkably stupid. So, altogether, I am not in the best of tempers. However, it comes to an end tomorrow afternoon, and perhaps Straus[1] and I may often have a good laugh together over the whole affair.

Another thing: rehearsals are quite out of the question, as there is no room and no time for them, so that nothing goes as it ought to do.

I suppose by now you are in Venice, and I need hardly say that I should be only too happy to come to you, but up to the present I hardly know what to say about it. I shall certainly not be able to leave London before the 12th or 13th, so much I see, and I have an absolute craving for some good music. I may say that it is a necessity for me to hear some good performances before beginning my work again, otherwise I might become a 'ganache', like so many others. So I meant to give myself a week or ten days of running in search of what may be interesting at Munich or Vienna, according to the répertoire; then, before coming back to England, I must spend a little more time at Hagen. . .

[To one of his daughters]

Hagen: July 22, 1884

I am still here. Yesterday evening, when my luggage had already been taken to the station, I felt that I could not tear myself away, and sent B. to fetch my bag back.

[1] Ludwig Straus was leader of the Hallé Orchestra from 1872 to 1888.

I shall never be able to give anybody an idea of what I feel here, of the immense longing for the past and for so many dear faces, all at rest. Not to speak of poor dear granny, I can stand before the house of Cornelius, vainly trying to persuade myself that I shall never see him again. I really think sometimes that I should feel happy if I could live here altogether, so you may imagine if I find it hard to go away.

Bayreuth: July 26, 1884

'Parsifal', yesterday, made a very deep impression upon me, much more so than before, and I shall see it again tomorrow with very great interest. After all, one has no idea in England of such a performance, and one ought to come here every year to learn what can be done—every detail is so perfect. The musical pleasure is not paramount, but there are very fine and powerful effects in it, and it is interesting throughout, and much less crude than 'Siegfried' and 'Tristan und Isolde'.

I have not seen Liszt yet and begin to doubt if I shall see him; the fact is, I don't like his *entourage*.

[To a friend]

Manchester: February 26, 1890

My dear ——[1]—I have been so terribly busy the last few days that I could not find a moment to write to you. Your last letter naturally interested me very much, and the Edinburgh outcry against me highly amused me. In the end people will see that I could not give up the Reid Festival without telling them the reason. Had I not done so, they would have imagined all sorts of reasons except the right one—viz., the bad attendance at the concerts. You know how often during the past three years I have spoken to you about the empty benches, and I should not have gone to Edinburgh this year had it not been the double jubilee. Now the public know the reason—the only reason—of my staying away, and with that I am content. For the rest, I said no word about 'want of appreciation', or of want of love for music,

---

[1] Almost certainly to Georg Lichstenstein. The Edinburgh critics had called Hallé's playing of the 'Emperor' 'arid and diffuse' and one had disparaged the concerto itself.

as you yourself can testify. That has been gratuitously attributed to me. I contented myself with the simple facts, and could not possibly add 'thanks for the bad attendance!' I now know that during the last few years the Professor contributed towards the expenses. When I wrote I felt sure of it, but had no positive proof. Can any one under such circumstances expect me to come again?

Also I cannot regret that I pounced upon the critics. They deserved it too richly, and one cannot *always* let them have the last word. That I had to attack your friend I am sorry for; but why did your friend never think into what a false position he put you through his ignorance and impudence? For *your* sake I am glad to have said what I did say, and on this point to have separated you from his stupidity. The frame of mind of such a man, who out of pure ignorance would, as it were, spit upon a work of art as divine as the Apollo Belvidere or the Venus of Milo, will ever remain incomprehensible to me. Respect for art, and the greatest masterpieces, I expect from every man, and from a so-called critic especially, and above all that the critic should have some knowledge of what to all men of the craft is irrefutable. Most likely the man in question never heard that both concertos, the E flat and the violin concerto, stand at an unattainable height. Oh, thou rhinoceros!

Why did you not educate him better? Warn him for his own sake.

But let us leave the Edinburghers alone, and let me rather ask you once again if you cannot come to one of my Manchester concerts? On March 6 we give 'Faust'. Make an escapade for once and come. It will give us great pleasure, and the performance will interest you very much. Write soon, and with kind regards to your ladies, believe me, ever

Your old friend,
Charles Hallé

[Extracts from a diary kept during a tour of Australia, 1890, with Lady Hallé]

Thursday, June 5, 1890

Yesterday morning Captain Briscoe paid us a visit, to our great surprise; he had only just arrived. He is to go to the concert with us this evening, and afterwards stay for supper. At 1.25 P.M. we left for Geelong, where we arrived at 3; were received by Mr. and Mrs. Poole, Otter and Rose, and drove to the 'Grand Coffee Palace'. Shortly after we had settled in our sitting-room a mouse descended by the window curtain and took up her quarters in a cottage piano, where later on we heard her rummaging amongst the wires. The view upon the harbour and the sea was rather fine. The concert at the Exhibition Theatre, a very draughty place, was crammed full, not a seat being vacant, and the applause was tumultuous. Geelong seems a very primitive place, and we had to walk through a long garden, into which carriages cannot enter, to get to the theatre. Fortunately, the weather was fine; if it had been raining we could hardly have got there at all. We left again at 10.45 this morning and arrived at Melbourne at 12. To-morrow we have a concert at Ballarat, and on Saturday here again; the one in Sandhurst is given up, or at all events postponed for the present.

Tuesday, June 10, 1890

The concert on Thursday last was again satisfactory in every respect. Friday morning we left for Ballarat, the celebrated gold-mining place. We arrived at 3 after a somewhat tedious journey through an uninteresting country, very thinly inhabited. Strange and weird-looking were a multitude of trees, bereft of all foliage and of all bark; they are killed by an incision made near the ground, called bark-ringing, after which they die, and in a year's time fall to the ground, thus saving the trouble of felling them. We found Craig's Royal Hotel a very small place, but the eating was much better than we expected. Ballarat lies 1,500 feet higher than Melbourne, and is therefore somewhat colder. It is a beautiful town, with broad streets and fine clean houses, most of them surrounded by splendid gardens. The concert was a curious affair, the house crammed to suffocation, in the cheaper places by crowds of miners who actually roared their applause. Unfortunately we had again much to suffer from draughts, the place being a theatre, and a rather dilapidated one; I was most anxious on account of Wilma, but fortunately she has not suffered much from it. On Saturday morning we left

207

again at 11 o'clock, but before then the President of the Associated Miners (himself one of them) and the Inspector of Mines called to present Wilma with a little piece of gold, as a memorial of Ballarat, and they offered, if we paid another visit to the place, to take us to the mines and show us everything worth seeing. We returned to Melbourne at 2.15, and had our eighth concert in the evening. A very full house again, and the usual success. The programmes had gone astray, and every piece had to be announced by Herr Scherch, the accompanist.

Sunday we spent at home, reading and writing letters to England, declining to see any visitors. Yesterday, Monday, Mr. Poole came to give me the dates of the first six concerts at Sydney, where he was going in the afternoon. The Chancellor of the University had invited me to meet him and the council at half-past 4 o'clock, which I did, and then aired my views about the Chair of Music. They seemed much impressed with what I had said, and asked me to revise the paper which they had sent out to candidates, and strike out those of the conditions I could not approve of, which I have promised to do. In the evening the Liedertafel gave me a reception, or a 'Social' as they call it, and presented me with a beautifully got-up address (to Sir Charles and Lady Hallé). The President, Judge Casey, is a very nice man, and the conductor, Mr. Hertz, extremely clever, to judge from the excellent way in which the Liedertafel, about 120 strong, sang. The quality of the voices, the ensemble and *nuances*, all were as good as could be wished for. All the evening I sat on a raised platform between the President and Baron von Müller, a celebrated botanist, who has been in Australia upwards of fifty years, and has explored it from east to west. It is curious that he and another gentleman, who was present last night, should have lived, fifty years ago, under a tent, in the midst of a bush and surrounded by kangaroos, on the very spot on which Melbourne stands now; so rapid has been the growth of the town. I made the acquaintance of Mr. Hayter, a Government Statist, who has sent me a most interesting book on the population of Victoria. It shows that before 1835 there was not one white man in the whole province, but about 5,000 aborigines; by May 25, 1836, there were 177 whites, by November 8 of the same year 224, two years later there were 3,511, and by April 3, 1881, 849,438. This shows what a new country it is; in 1841 there were in the whole province only 1,490 dwellings, and in 1881 their number was 179,816. The population of Melbourne falls short of that of Manchester, without Salford, and the wonder is that so many concerts can be given in so short a time; but then, there are no poor people here at all, and a beggar is not known.

To-day is a good day for practice, and I must say that the contact with a new public has done us much good, and has put fresh musical life into us. Playing so constantly in England as we do, it becomes a matter of routine, and loses its interest; here we are quite astonished to find that we take a real interest in every concert, in every article in the papers, and we certainly do our very best. It is a great satisfaction to witness the breathless attention with which these large crowds listen to us; there is not the least exaggeration in saying that you might hear a pin drop; and never a soul stirs before the last note is played.

June 11, 1890

The concert last night was full, without being crowded. The wretched weather must have detained many. Mr. Wilson, from Ballarat, a son of the late Canon Wilson, of Manchester, this morning sent Wilma a box full of specimens from the different gold mines; they are extremely interesting and gave her much pleasure. Two gentlemen travelled 500 miles yesterday to hear us and are returning to-day, but wish to shake hands before they leave. . .

[From a letter written during a tour of South Africa, 1895]

Johannesburg: September 1, 1895

My last letter actually, for the next mail will carry ourselves home after a wonderfully interesting, successful, and very short trip. One of my greatest pleasures has been, of course, to spend a whole fortnight with Gus.[1]

Since last I wrote we have been twice to Pretoria, and here we give this evening, Sunday evening, our fifth concert. On our

---

[1] His son Gustave, who had emigrated to South Africa.

second visit to Pretoria I was introduced to President Krüger by his Prime Minister, and found him an ugly but very energetic-looking man, in manners a real Boer. I shall give details when I see you. Altogether, I need not write much to-day, because one week after you receive this I can tell you all so much better.

Yesterday we went down a gold mine, one of the best here, took luncheon with Gus, and in the evening went to the theatre to see a stupid but very laughable and well-acted farce. To-day (I write early) we shall see a Kaffir dance, got up entirely in our honour, about which I shall add a few words before closing my letter. The dance is fixed for 11 o'clock; at half-past one we take luncheon with Mr. and Mrs. Rogers (he is one of the most important men here), where there will be a garden party in the afternoon and the concert begins at 9 o'clock to-night. The weather is always the same, the sky intensely blue, without a single cloud, the days very warm, and the nights somewhat fresh. Johannesburg has, however, one great drawback: the dust, which lies at least 3 inches deep in every street and every road. We have had one windy day, when the clouds of dust were extraordinary to look at and certainly not pleasant. We had quite enough with that one day, and fortunately have not experienced a second.

We leave to-morrow at twelve, and arrive at Bloemfontein after midnight (by rail, of course), and give a concert there on Tuesday. On Wednesday we go to Kimberley, have concerts there on Thursday and Friday; shall visit the biggest diamond mine, and on Saturday leave for Cape Town, where we give a farewell concert on Tuesday, the 10th, and on the 11th we go on board the *Scot*. . .

We have just come back from the dance, a most extraordinary wild scene it was. There were about 1,000 Kaffirs and Zulus, well-armed with long sticks instead of assegais, singing their war songs, dancing and rushing about in the most bewildering manner, and still always orderly. They gave us tremendous salutes, and when the performance was half over, the chief, a most noble-looking fellow, walked up and was introduced to Wilma, and said some nice things which were translated to her. Altogether it was worth coming to Africa for; we could never have got an idea of it elsewhere.

And now, *au revoir* very soon. We are as well as possible, and

210

have enjoyed ourselves thoroughly. I hope the house is in tip-top order, and that the building at the College will be finished in good time.[1]

---

[1] Some extensions to the Royal Manchester College of Music, which had opened in 1893 and was already in need of extra accommodation.

INDEX

213